Why?

*Trusting God
When You Don't Understand*

*Also by Anne Graham Lotz
in Large Print:*

Heaven: My Father's House

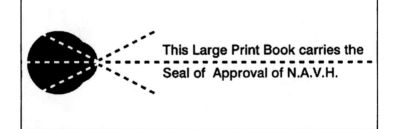

Why?

Trusting God
When You Don't Understand

Anne Graham Lotz

CHRISTIAN LARGE PRINT
A part of Gale, Cengage Learning

GALE
CENGAGE Learning

Detroit • New York • San Francisco • New Haven, Conn • Waterville, Maine • London

GALE
CENGAGE Learning·

Published in 2005 by arrangement with Thomas Nelson, Inc.

The text of this Large Print edition is unabridged.
Other aspects of the book may vary from the original edition.

Set in 16 pt. Plantin by Liana M. Walker.

Printed on permanent paper.

The Library of Congress has cataloged the Thorndike Press ® edition as follows:

Lotz, Anne Graham, 1948–
    Why? : trusting God when you don't understand /
    by Anne Graham Lotz.
        p. cm.
    Includes bibliographical references.
    ISBN 0-7862-7147-7 (lg. print : hc : alk. paper)
    ISBN 1-59415-064-8 (lg. print : sc : alk. paper)
    1. Consolation. 2. Large type books. I. Title.
BV4905.3.L68 2005
248.8´6—dc22   2004059869

Printed in the United States of America
    2 3 4 5 6   12 11 10 09 08
ED254

*Dedicated
to
those who have unanswered prayers*

As the Founder/CEO of NAVH, the only national health agency solely devoted to those who, although not totally blind, have an eye disease which could lead to serious visual impairment, I am pleased to recognize Thorndike Press* as one of the leading publishers in the large print field.

Founded in 1954 in San Francisco to prepare large print textbooks for partially seeing children, NAVH became the pioneer and standard setting agency in the preparation of large type.

Today, those publishers who meet our standards carry the prestigious "Seal of Approval" indicating high quality large print. We are delighted that Thorndike Press is one of the publishers whose titles meet these standards. We are also pleased to recognize the significant contribution Thorndike Press is making in this important and growing field.

Lorraine H. Marchi, L.H.D.
Founder/CEO
NAVH

* Thorndike Press encompasses the following imprints: Thorndike, Wheeler, Walker and Large Print Press.

Contents

In a Difficult Place,
a Strange, Warm Peace . . .

Before my husband and I rushed out the door yesterday to drive my mother-in-law to UCLA's cancer clinic, I rummaged around looking for reading material to help bide the time. "Here, take this," my friend said, handing me a manuscript that had just arrived in the mail. I looked at the title, *Why?* and remembered I had promised Anne Graham Lotz I would write the foreword. I tucked it in my bag, and we were off.

We arrived at the clinic and had to search for a few open seats. The place was crowded with families sitting quietly, somberly flipping through maga-zines, and checking their watches every now and then. The air was heavy with sadness. I glanced at my mother-in-law, a frail eighty-four-year-old woman struggling against the last stages of pancreatic cancer. She sat slumped, waiting, with both hands folded on top of her purse. My heart twisted whenever I saw her wince in pain. All of us were hoping she'd be helped with one more chemotherapy treatment.

I breathed a prayer as they escorted Mom Tada — that's what I've always affectionately called this brave, hardy little Japanese woman — into the chemo room. She hunched her shoul-ders, and I could tell the pain was worse. *Oh, Lord Jesus,* I prayed, *can You not lighten her load a bit? Ease her plight? Please?*

After Ken and his mother disap-peared behind the doors, I sighed and turned to Anne's manuscript and began reading.

After the first five pages, I sensed a strange, warm peace flood my heart. The Bible verses seemed fresh and alive. The story of Mary, Martha, and Lazarus — I felt as though I were reading it for the first time. The testimonies were riveting and revealing. The poems and quotes resonated. Page after page, I found comfort and consolation, encouragement and insight. I looked up and bit my lip, realizing God was using this remarkable book, *Why?* to speak to me, to comfort me, to escort me into the deeper recesses of the heart of my Savior.

God, thank You for placing this book in my hands for such a moment as this!

Mom Tada's chemo treatment took almost three hours. By the time she was wheeled back into the waiting room, I had nearly finished the manuscript. Breathing a sigh and sharing my smile, I gave my mother-in-law a hug straight from the heart. Or maybe . . . it was a hug straight from God's heart. For Anne Graham Lotz had helped me "get it all back in focus." Her book *Why?* provided just the insight, just the comfort, I needed to pass on to my family that afternoon. Bolstered and boosted by the Spirit of Christ, we sang hymns all the way back home.

Need I say more about the book you hold in your hands?

Thank you, Anne, for reminding me — for reminding us all — that we can trust the One Who holds all the answers to that jarring question *Why?* Just knowing that is . . . enough.

JONI EARECKSON TADA
Joni and Friends
winter 2004

. . . And a Word of Comfort and Hope

This book is based on the following portion of God's Word:

Now a man named Lazarus was sick. He was from Bethany, the village of Mary and her sister Martha. This Mary, whose brother Lazarus now lay sick, was the same one who poured perfume on the Lord and wiped his feet with her hair. So the sisters sent word to Jesus, "Lord, the one you love is sick."

When he heard this, Jesus said, "This sickness will not end in death. No, it is for God's glory so that God's Son may be glorified through it." Jesus loved Martha and her sister and Lazarus. Yet when he heard that Lazarus was sick, he stayed where he was two more days.

Then he said to his disciples, "Let us go back to Judea."

"But Rabbi," they said, "a short while ago the Jews tried to stone you, and yet you are going back there?"

Jesus answered, "Are there not twelve hours of daylight? A man who walks by day will not stumble, for he sees by this world's light. It is when he walks by night that he stumbles, for he has no light."

After he had said this, he went on to tell them, "Our friend Lazarus has fallen asleep; but I am going there to wake him up."

His disciples replied, "Lord, if he sleeps, he will get better." Jesus had been speaking of his death, but his disciples thought he meant natural sleep.

So then he told them plainly, "Lazarus is dead, and for your sake I am glad I was not there, so that you may believe. But let us go to him."

Then Thomas (called Didymus) said to the rest of the disciples, "Let us also go, that we may die with him."

On his arrival, Jesus found that Lazarus had already been in the tomb for four days. Bethany was less than two miles from Jerusalem, and many Jews had come to Martha and Mary to comfort them in the loss of their brother. When Martha heard that Jesus was coming, she went out to meet him, but Mary stayed at home.

"Lord," Martha said to Jesus, "if you had been here, my brother would not have died. But I know that even now God will give you whatever you ask."

Jesus said to her, "Your brother will rise again."

Martha answered, "I know he will rise again in the resurrection at the last day."

Jesus said to her, "I am the resurrection and the life. He who believes in me will live, even though he dies; and whoever lives and believes in me will never die. Do you believe this?"

"Yes, Lord," she told him, "I believe that you are the Christ, the Son of God, who was to come into the world."

And after she had said this, she went back and called her sister Mary aside. "The Teacher is here," she said, "and is asking for you." When Mary heard this, she got up quickly and went to him. Now Jesus had not yet entered the village, but was still at the place where Martha had met him. When the Jews who had been with Mary in the house, comforting her, noticed how quickly she got up and went out, they followed her, supposing she was going to the tomb to mourn there.

When Mary reached the place where Jesus was and saw him, she fell at his feet and said, "Lord, if you had been here, my brother would not have died."

When Jesus saw her weeping, and the Jews who had come along with her also weeping, he was deeply moved in spirit and troubled. "Where have you laid him?" he asked.

"Come and see, Lord," they replied.

Jesus wept.

Then the Jews said, "See how he loved him!"

But some of them said, "Could not he who opened the eyes of the blind man have kept this man from dying?"

Jesus, once more deeply moved, came to the tomb. It was a cave with a stone laid across the entrance. "Take away the stone," he said.

"But, Lord," said Martha, the sister

of the dead man, "by this time there is a bad odor, for he has been there four days."

Then Jesus said, "Did I not tell you that if you believed, you would see the glory of God?"

So they took away the stone. Then Jesus looked up and said, "Father, I thank you that you have heard me. I knew that you always hear me, but I said this for the benefit of the people standing here, that they may believe that you sent me."

When he had said this, Jesus called in a loud voice, "Lazarus, come out!" The dead man came out, his hands and feet wrapped with strips of linen, and a cloth around his face.

Jesus said to them, "Take off the grave clothes and let him go."

I lay my "whys?"
before Your cross
in worship kneeling,
my mind beyond all hope,
my heart beyond all feeling;
and worshipping,
realize that I
in knowing You,
don't need a "why?"

— RUTH BELL GRAHAM

Why?

*Trusting God
When I Don't Understand*

Trust in the LORD with all your heart
and lean not on your own
understanding.

— PROVERBS 3:5

Why? Why does God let bad things happen to good people?

    to innocent people?

      to helpless people?

        to defenseless people?

          to children?

        to *me?*

Sometimes His ways seem so hard to understand!

What I have to share in this small volume comes from what I have learned through experience as each lesson was hammered out on the anvil of God's Word. While I have not known suffering to the extent others have endured — I have not suffered the death of a child, the betrayal or abandonment of a spouse, or an illness that threatened my own life — my own problems, added to my interactions with hurting people around the globe and my intense study to understand how God works and what He has to say about suffering, give me courage to speak to those hurting ones who struggle to understand *why.*

Through all these avenues, realizing there are no pat answers to the age-old question of suffering, and no "new truth," I cling to the spiritual principle operating in the life of a child of God that . . .
gives meaning to our meaninglessness
and hope to our hopelessness
and reason to our senselessness
and purpose to our aimlessness
and strength to our weakness
and courage to our faintheartedness
and blessed deliverance from our bitterness.
It's a principle . . .
that helps balance the pain,
that can remove the sting from our suffering,
that can prevent us from wasting our sorrows,
that is worth our focused attention.
This spiritual principle is seen when a single grain of wheat is crushed, buried, and, in a

sense, dies — only to rise again into new life as the stalk of wheat grows from it, producing hundreds more grains. This principle emerged into sharp visibility when Jesus gave His life on the Cross, was buried, and on the third day arose from the dead to give eternal life to any and all who would place their faith in Him.

On a day still to come, this same principle will be thrillingly displayed when the intense suffering that characterizes the final generation in human history gives "birth" to the glorious return to earth of God's Son and our Savior, Jesus Christ.[1]

The apostle Paul somewhat understated this principle in Romans 8:28, a passage he wrote to reassure believers who lived in a city dominated by Nero, a madman with absolute power. Paul wrote encouragingly, "We know that in all things God works for the good of those who love him, who have been called according to his purpose."

Phrased another way, Paul was reminding the children of God they can be confident that . . .

all things work together for good,
  brokenness leads to blessing,
    death leads to life,[2]
      and suffering leads to glory![3]

In our world today, God's children need

that same reminder to trust Him when we don't understand and nothing seems to make sense.

Nowhere is this principle taught more poignantly or powerfully than in the passage of Scripture on which this book is based, the Gospel of John, chapter 11. (Direct quotations from John 11 are inserted in the text; other Scripture references can be found in the Notes section.) In this passage, the apostle John gives his eyewitness account of the moving story of Lazarus, a beloved friend of Jesus who became seriously ill. It's also the story of Lazarus's two sisters, Mary and Martha, who struggled to understand why Jesus hadn't intervened and healed their brother. While both sisters sent word to Jesus, Mary's faith seemed to collapse when things got worse while Martha's small tendril of faith was developed until she saw the glory of God in her brother's life. Because I identify with Martha's struggle, I have chosen to focus primarily on her perspective in this book. Through the apostle John's eyes, as I see Martha's faith in God grow in the midst of her total helplessness until it becomes triumphant — even a model for my own — my desire is increased for that kind of faith.

Similarly, believers of every generation have triumphed over their suffering as they placed their faith in God, trusting Him even when they didn't understand why. And every generation *has* suffered to a greater or lesser degree.

My generation has not been exempt.

There has been unfathomable hopelessness and helplessness in the killing fields of Cambodia under the Khmer Rouge, in the massacres under the vicious anarchy of the Red Guard in China, in the senseless slaughter between tribes in Rwanda, in the torture chambers supervised by the Butcher of Baghdad, in the slave trade of the Sudan, in the systematic ethnic cleansing of Eastern Europe, and in countless acts of cruelty and sadism that never make it to the light of national or international attention. While writing this book, I have had in my heart and on my mind the millions of people *today* who are suffering personally in various ways and to varying degrees. *Why?* Sometimes it's just so hard to understand!

Yet God is bigger than our suffering. We can have hope as we place our trust in Him — in His faithfulness and in His ability to work out in our lives His purposes that will be for our ultimate good and His eternal glory.

Although Mary and Martha experienced suffering and prayers that were seemingly unanswered, in the end their faith was gloriously rewarded, teaching us just to trust Him when we don't understand.

The principle that suffering leads to glory is illustrated in Scripture by a vivid description of clay on the Potter's wheel — clay that was once cracked, shattered, and broken, clay that was totally useless and ugly. The Potter took the clay and broke it down even further, grinding it into dust then moistening it with water before He put it on His wheel and began to remake it into a vessel pleasing to Himself. The cracks and chips and broken pieces disappeared as the clay became soft and pliable to the Potter's touch. He firmly applied pressure on some areas, touched lightly on other areas, added more clay to a specific spot that needed filling, and removed clay that hindered the shape that would make it useful for His ultimate purpose. As He turned the wheel, His loving, gentle hands never left the clay as He molded and made it after His will.

Finally, the Potter finished remolding the clay and took it off the wheel. Under His skilled, gentle hands, the once-ugly clay had been transformed into a vessel that had shape and purpose. He added color, carefully painting on a unique design. But the clay was still soft and weak, the color dull and drab. So the Potter placed the vessel into the fiery kiln, carefully keeping His eye on it as He submitted it to the raging heat. At a time He alone determined was sufficient, the Potter withdrew the pot from the furnace. The blazing heat had radically transformed the clay into a vessel of strength and glorious, multicolored beauty. Then the Potter put it in His showcase so that others might see the revelation of His glory in the work of His hands.[4]

Is the Potter molding — or remolding — you, using . . .

pressure or problems?
stress or suffering?
hurt or heartache?
illness or injustice?

Has He now placed you in the fire so that circumstances are heating up with intensity in your life? Then would you just trust the Potter to know exactly what He is doing?

For the child of God, suffering is not wasted. It's not an end in itself. Scripture reminds us, "We have this treasure in jars of clay to show that this all-surpassing power is from God and not from us. We are hard pressed on every side, but not crushed; perplexed, but not in despair; persecuted, but not abandoned; struck down, but not destroyed. We always carry around in our body the death of Jesus, so that the life of Jesus may also be revealed in our body. . . . For our light and momentary troubles are achieving for us an eternal glory that far outweighs them all."[5]

The spiritual principle is that in some way God uses suffering to transform ordinary, dust-clay people into . . .

vessels that are strong in faith . . .
vessels that are fit for His use . . .
vessels that display His glory to the watching world.

This is the principle so powerfully illustrated in the story of Mary, Martha, and Lazarus in John 11. I also have seen this principle at work personally — in the lives of family members and friends. And I understand it to be true by my own experience.

When I don't understand why, I trust Him because . . .

Why Doesn't God Care?

Trusting God's Heart

I pray that you,
being rooted and established in love,
may have power,
together with all the saints,
to grasp how wide and long
and high and deep
is the love of Christ,
and to know this love
that surpasses knowledge —
that you may be filled to the measure
of all the fullness of God.

— EPHESIANS 3:17–19

My mother's pale, gaunt face was transformed into wreaths of joy when I walked through the door of her hospital room. Although her eyes seemed sunken, they sparkled with the zest for life that is her own special trademark. With IVs dangling from her arms, she lifted her trembling hands to welcome me. I embraced her frail body, feeling the heat of her temperature and the protrusion of her bones through the thin hospital gown. She was unable to speak clearly, so I just patted her and sat down nearby. Within moments, she was asleep. And I was left to wonder, *Why?* Why does my mother's life seem to be ending in suffering and, at times, confusion? Why, after a life lived selflessly for others, must her old age be, in some ways, a curse?

Yet I was reminded that unanswerable questions are not restricted to any particular age group when my son recently went through a series of tests to determine his physical condition five years after cancer surgery. The *why's* buzz through my head like irritating mental insects: *Why? Why is my handsome, six-foot-nine-inch, thirty-two-year-old son still stalked by the shadow of this horrific disease?*

While wrestling with the illnesses of my mother and son, a beloved young friend was entering into the living death that is divorce. *Why?* Why doesn't God melt the heart of the offending spouse and bring that person to genuine repentance so the marriage can be saved?

And once again, the angel of death has struck, this time taking the life of the beloved pastor who ministered to my family and shepherded me through my formative years. *Why?*

And before that personal loss, I had other *why's.*

Why would God allow 110 fathers of unborn children to perish in the collapse of the Twin Towers on September 11, 2001?

Why would God withhold children from godly parents and give them to a mother who would bash in their heads with a rock or drown them in a bathtub?

Why would God allow thousands of people to lose their pensions because of greedy corporate executives who are padding their own retirement fortunes?

Why would God allow men, in His Name, to abuse innocent children . . . and continue in ministry?

Why would God allow politicians, athletes, entertainers, and other celebrities to profit from their sin? And increase their profits as they openly flaunt their immorality and wickedness?

Why would God allow the kidnapping of innocent babies and children for the perverted pleasure of some pedophile?

Why do the young die?

Why do the godly perish?

Why do the wicked prosper?

What, or who, has . . .

> turned on the tap of your tears,
> and tossed you in your bed at night,
> and preoccupied your waking thoughts,
> and blackened your hopes for the future,
> and broken your heart,

and wrenched an agonized "Why?" from your trembling lips?

Broken hearts asking the question *Why?* are as old as the human race, beginning with our first parents. What would it have been like to wake up the morning after having been banished from the Garden of Eden because of a very wrong choice? I would imagine Adam and Eve had been lying on the cold, hard ground, covered in smelly animal skins. After dark hours of fitful sleep, did they have a moment in between unconsciousness and full alertness when they thought everything they had been through the day before was just a horrible nightmare — only to come fully awake and face to face with the cold, hard consequences of their choice to disobey God? They would have found no comfort in each other that night after the way Eve had involved Adam in her sin — and Adam had blamed Eve when convicted of it. They may not even have been speaking to each other!

In utter loneliness, separated and alienated from God, their minds must have initially been preoccupied with reliving those awful moments that had led to their disobedience.

Why did I talk to the snake?

Why didn't I pray first?
Why didn't God intervene to protect us?

The most tragic day in all of human history could not be relived. And the tragedy was not over. In the years to come, after the joy of giving birth to three sons, their hearts were broken once again as Adam and Eve buried their second son, who was murdered by their firstborn.

Why?

God answered what surely was their unspoken question with a promise that transcended the generations for every age to come when He reassured Adam and Eve that one day He would send a Savior Who would destroy the power of sin, death, and the devil — the fundamental sources of all human suffering.[1] Ultimately this brokenness did lead to blessing, and their suffering did lead to glory when Jesus Christ, their descendant in the flesh, came to redeem mankind from sin and reconcile the world to God. To our heart-wrenched cries of *Why?* God's ultimate answer is, "Jesus," as He is glorified and magnified in our lives through our suffering.[2] Trust Him. When guilt takes the edge off every joy . . .

When there are no answers to your
        questions . . .
    Trust Him when you don't

understand.
Trust His heart.
Trust His purpose.
Trust Him when it is your heart that's broken.
Trust His goodness.
Trust Him beyond the grave.
Trust Him to know best.
Trust His plan to be bigger than yours.
Trust Him to keep His Word.
Trust Him to be on time.
Trust Him to be enough.
Trust Him to set you free.
Trust Him — and Him alone!

The times when you and I can't trace His hand of purpose, we must trust His heart of love! *Trust HIM!*

When I don't understand why, I trust Him because . . .

*God does care —
more than I can possibly know.*

Why Does God Let Bad Things Happen?

Trusting God's Purpose

The burden of suffering
seems a tombstone
hung about our necks,
while in reality it is only the weight
which is necessary
to keep down the diver
while he is hunting for pearls.

— JEAN PAUL RICHTER

When the telephone rang on February 26, 1998, I had no idea the call would precipitate a launch into the wild blue yonder of faith. My son's voice on the other end of the line sounded strong but serious. "Mom, the doctor thinks I have cancer."

With those few words, I was suddenly catapulted into the eye of an unexpected, raging storm of suffering that lashed at every aspect of my life.

One of my priorities as a mother has been to make sure my children are safe. When they were small, I carefully strapped them into their car seats, held their hands protectively when walking, made sure the medicines and cleaning products were safely out of reach, and barricaded the steps or other areas where they might hurt themselves. As they grew up, I made sure I knew who their friends were, where they spent their time, and what they were being taught in school. I carefully helped them select television programs, movies, and reading material that would be fun and stimulating but would not damage their minds or spirits. I gave them prayerful, thoughtful counsel on their choice of where to go to college, whom to marry, what jobs to take, and where to live. But what could I do in the face of cancer? Never have I felt so helpless!

Yet in the midst of the storm that hit as suddenly and fiercely as a devastating tornado, I experienced an unprecedented peace — and joy! Because I knew that while I was helpless in myself, I could lay hold of One Who is mighty and Whose faithfulness surrounds Him.[1] So, with tears streaming down my cheeks, I prayed with my son, Jonathan, on the telephone during that initial conversation. I was able to praise God for His divine purpose for Jonathan's life, which apparently included cancer. Although we had been caught by surprise, I knew God had known about it since before Jonathan was born. I knew also that Jonathan had been prayed for before conception, every day of my pregnancy, and every day of his life since birth. He had been born again into God's family as a child, and now as a young adult he was in God's will as far as he understood it. Therefore I had absolute confidence that this suffering would be for Jonathan's good and God's glory.[2] We *knew* God had a plan, and apparently cancer was part of it!

So, on the telephone, Jonathan and I prayed together, recommitting his life for the purpose of glorifying God. We acknowledged that he could bring God glory through faithfully trusting Him if the cancer led to death . . . or if the cancer went into remission . . . or if the cancer was surgically and successfully removed . . . or if the cancer simply disappeared. When I hung up the telephone with tears on my face and a lump in my throat and an ache in my heart, I knew I was soaring higher in faith than I ever had before.

In the next few hours, which seemed like years, the doctor's diagnosis was confirmed by the examination of a specialist. Within a week of the first diagnosis, and just four weeks before his wedding day, our twenty-eight-year-old son underwent successful surgery to remove a malignant tumor. After completing the recommended follow-up treatments of radiation, Jonathan's prognosis for total recovery has been excellent.

As grateful and thrilled as we still are over this answer to our prayers, the real victory was won, not on the surgeon's table, but on the telephone, in prayer, as we agreed to trust God with whatever the outcome might be.

What bad thing, what storm of suffering, has swept into *your* life, rendering you helpless? The storm of

death?

divorce?

disease?

debt?

Instead of being delivered, did your loved one die from cancer? Has . . .

a feud erupted in your family?

a betrayal occurred in your
marriage?

a rebellion challenged your
parenting?

an untimely end come to your
pregnancy?

a severance taken you from your job?

a military deployment deprived you of
your loved one?

Besides feeling totally helpless, what has

been your reaction to the storm? Are you defiantly standing in the midst of the swirling circumstances, yelling in your spirit, *Why did You let this bad thing happen?* Or maybe you are withdrawing into a shell of denial and depression, hoping the storm won't get any worse.

Even smaller storms of stress can be overwhelming when clustered together, becoming one large, collective storm of suffering. Within a period of eighteen months, I went through just such a cluster of storms that left me emotionally gasping for breath. From Hurricane Fran, which downed 102 trees in our yard, to the fire that consumed my husband's dental office, to Jonathan's cancer and surgery, to my parents' increasingly fragile health that has included multiple hospitalizations, to a home remodeling project that involved a contractor who took our money but refused to do the work, I reeled from one emergency or crisis to another. On top of these stresses, we celebrated the joyful but exhausting weddings of *all three of our children* within eight months of each other! In the whirlwind, I found myself wanting to withdraw from the aching pain and burdensome demands and frenzied activities and unending responsibilities. I wanted to run and hide from friends and family who felt ignored or slighted, misunderstanding my busyness and preoccupation for indifference or arrogance. I crouched in my spirit from the verbal cheerleaders who exhorted me to be strong, or from the analytical critics who concluded it was my fault. I wanted to escape the hurt.

I understand that a turkey and an eagle react differently to the threat of a storm. A turkey reacts by running under the barn, hoping the storm won't come near. On the other hand, an eagle leaves the security of its nest and spreads its wings to ride the air currents of the approaching storm, knowing they will carry it higher in the sky than it could soar on its own. Based on your reaction to the storms of life, which are you? A turkey or an eagle?

It's natural for me to be a turkey in my emotions, but I have chosen to be an eagle in my spirit. And as I have spread my wings of faith to embrace the "Wind,"[3] placing my trust in Jesus and Jesus alone, I have experienced quiet, "everyday" miracles:

His joy has balanced my pain.

His power has lifted my burden.

His peace has calmed my worries.

His grace has been more than

adequate to cover me.
His strength has been sufficient to
carry me through.
His love has bathed my wounds
like a healing balm.

Soaring has become an adventure of discovering just how faithful He can be when I am way out of my comfort zone in the stratosphere over the storm. Soaring is an adventure of discovering by experience His answer to my pain. And I imagine a smile of infinite tenderness on His face as the angels in heaven applaud, "Anne, you're finally getting it. Now you're beginning to understand one of the reasons why God has allowed these bad things to happen."

And, to a greater degree than ever before, I do understand. Soaring is so exhilarating, I find increasingly that I am no longer content to live in the barnyard of familiar comfort just for the relative security that seems to be there. I want to live by faith! I want to live in . . .

barrier-breaking,
mountain-moving,
sea-parting,
sun-stopping,
river-drying,
fire-falling,

triumphant faith!

Looking back over that eighteen-month period, my thoughtful, confident conclusion is that God allowed the storms of suffering to increase and intensify in my life because He wanted me to soar higher in my relationship with Him —

to fall deeper in love with Him,
to grow stronger in my faith in Him,
to be more consistent in my walk with Him,
to bear more fruit in my service to Him,
to draw closer to His heart,
to keep my focus on His face,
to live for His glory alone!

Faith that triumphantly soars is possible only when the winds of life are contrary to personal comfort.[4] That kind of faith is His ultimate purpose in allowing us to encounter storms of suffering. Trust Him!

Jesus taught us this lesson of triumphant faith in the little town of Bethany in the days that immediately preceded the . . .

history-splitting,
death-defying,
grave-robbing,
heaven-opening

storm that broke in Jesus' own life at Calvary — a storm that carried Him to the very highest pinnacle of glory and power. In that

48

small-town setting, Jesus revealed God's answer to our question, "Why did You let this bad thing happen?" His timeless response to our heartfelt query was given dramatically and unforgettably to Mary, Martha, and Lazarus — a family living in Bethany. Ultimately they soared to the very heights of faith on the wings of the storm that suddenly swept into their lives. As we will see in the pages ahead, their experience underscores the truth that God's picture for our lives is much bigger than our own. And it reminds us of the challenge to simply trust His greater purpose when bad things happen.

When I don't understand why, I trust Him because . . .

God can lift me up to soar
above the storms in my life.

Why Me?

Trusting God When It's
My Heart That's Broken

I have learnt to love
the darkness of sorrow;
there you see
the brightness
of His face.

— MADAME GUYON

Everyone knows that bad things happen. But it can be so easy, when some bad thing smashes *my* heart or the heart of someone *I* love, to impulsively respond, "Why did God let this happen? What have I done wrong? Is He displeased with me?" The unspoken thought is that if God really loved me, if my life was truly pleasing to Him, if everything was "all right" between us, only good things would happen to me, because a loving heavenly Father surely wants me, as His child, to be healthy, wealthy, happy, and problem free. So when a bad thing happens, nagging questions about my relationship with Him begin to surface and actually intensify my misery.

I need to be reminded that that logical,

yet inaccurate, thought process is emphatically contradicted by the apostle John's eyewitness account of what happened to the family in Bethany. It was a startlingly phenomenal event that provoked the enemies of Jesus Christ and propelled them to move against Him in a radical way. John introduced the event by stating simply, "A man named Lazarus was sick. He was from Bethany, the village of Mary and her sister Martha" (11:1).

Bethany was a small town on the southeastern slope of the Mount of Olives, just two miles from Jerusalem. The hot, dusty streets and organized piles of stone that served as houses made Bethany virtually indistinguishable from other villages of its day — with one notable exception. The exception was that Jesus, in effect, considered Bethany His second home. It was a place where He relaxed and retreated from the pressures and demands of ministry. It was the starting place of His triumphal entry into Jerusalem, and later it would be the departing point for His ascension into heaven. Each night during His final week before the Cross, after teaching in the temple all day, Jesus and His disciples would slip over to Bethany to rest and be refreshed. What gave it such favor in His eyes? The main attraction seemed to be a particular home in which He felt comfortable

and at ease
and loved
and accepted
and honored
and enjoyed
and trusted.

This place of refuge was the home of a well-to-do family that included Lazarus and his sisters, Mary and Martha.[1] It was in this place of refuge, during the turmoil of Lazarus's illness and death, that the apostle John described the dramatic transformation of Lazarus's sister Martha as she chose to stop being a "turkey," left the barnyard of doubting questions, and soared on eagles' wings of faith.

I assume Martha was the eldest because she was like my older sister — bossy! She was bustling, energetic, practical, and always seemed to be in charge. But she was known to get so caught up in the details of her responsibilities that she would lose her focus.[2] The Gospel writer Luke revealed that when Martha threw a dinner party, she got so busy preparing the meal she didn't enjoy the guests when they came. Jesus, one of those guests, gently rebuked her when He pointed out she was busy about so many things, yet she was missing the best part, which was to enjoy Him.[3] Yet the apostle John noted, "Jesus loved Martha" (11:5).

Martha's sister, Mary, was intuitively sensitive, deeply spiritual, and thoughtfully quiet. She seemed like a still pool that runs deep. In spite of household demands, she made the time to sit at Jesus' feet and listen to His Word, a trait for which she received His encouraging, lasting commendation.[4] She was devoted to Him. She "was the same one who poured perfume on the Lord and wiped his feet with her hair" (11:2). Just as Jesus loved Martha, He loved Mary too (11:5).

It has been suggested that Mary and Martha's brother, Lazarus, may have been the rich young ruler who asked Jesus how he could get to heaven. When Jesus replied he would have to give up everything and follow Him in a life of costly discipleship, the young man turned away sadly because he had many possessions.[5] Yet three times in John 11 we're told that Jesus loved Lazarus (vv. 3, 5, 36). If Lazarus was indeed that same young ruler who had chosen his personal wealth over discipleship, it makes this astounding story an even more powerful and poignant display of God's grace and mercy.

This beloved family is also assumed to be wealthy because they had their own burial cave, they had been capable of putting on a large dinner party in Jesus' honor, and Mary had a jar of very costly perfume. But John's introduction to their story — "Lazarus was sick" — shows that neither their wealth, nor their position in the community, nor their friends, nor their love for each other, nor their love of God was able to protect them from suffering.

I recently talked with a woman who is as lovely as anyone I have ever met. She is beautiful, poised, educated, articulate, and wealthy. Expensive restaurants that bear her family name are sprinkled throughout the region. But tears filled her eyes as she told me about the infidelity of her son-in-law and the birth of her physically challenged granddaughter. And as I grieved with her and prayed for her, I was reminded that pain and suffering cross all boundaries of society, economics, race, culture, gender, religion, region, education, and language. And ultimate suffering, which is death, is the ultimate equalizer.

What did you think would protect you from suffering? When pain has penetrated your sphere of existence, have you become angry, resentful, and confused as to how this possibly could happen to *you?* Have you asked why this bad thing happened to you? Have you doubted God's love for you personally? Are you mentally wandering in confusion as you seek to determine what you have done that was so bad as to deserve *this?*

The well-to-do family of three in Bethany that was so beloved by Jesus experienced a bad thing when Lazarus became ill. His sickness was surely more than a summer cold or virus. Perhaps he was stricken with a high fever and splitting migraine headache and severe dysentery. As he grew weaker and paler, fear and helplessness must have gripped the little family. Think how they must have felt. Their loved one was desperately ill, but there were no . . .

sterile hospitals
or high-tech x-rays
or expensive lab tests
or even nurses in squeaky white shoes.

There were no . . .

thermometers
or stethoscopes
or pain relievers
or antibiotics.

With all their wealth and influence, Mary, Martha, and Lazarus were helpless in the face of this silent attacker. They became so alarmed in their helpless state that "the sisters sent word to Jesus, 'Lord, the one you love is sick' " (11:3). When something bad happened to their little family, they desperately cried out for help. They knew they needed Jesus. Their unspoken plea must have been, "Please, Jesus, do something! Now! Help! *If You really do love us,* come and make Lazarus well."

When have you felt so totally helpless that your prayer was fathoms deeper than mere words — it was a desperate heart's cry? Was it when some bad thing happened to someone you love? Was it when you experienced . . .

a physical illness?

a financial collapse?

a severed relationship?

social rejection?

a religious exclusion?

a family betrayal?

an emotional abuse?

Did you think because something bad happened, it indicated Jesus doesn't really know what's going on? Or that maybe He knows, but He's not pleased with you? Or that *if* He does know, He just doesn't love you or your family enough to do anything about it? Are you interpreting His love *by your circumstances* instead of interpreting your circumstances *by His love?* Did you forget God's most astounding revelation, that He "so loved the world that he gave his only Son"?[6] For this very reason, when we are tempted to question whether or not God cares, we are reminded that "God demonstrates his own love for us in this: While we were still sinners, Christ died for us."[7] He cares! *God does care!* Maybe that's one reason why this passage from John's Gospel repeats again and again that each member of this family was loved by Jesus. Because bad things *do happen* to those Jesus loves. But remember the spiritual principle: Glory follows suffering, and life follows death. It's a principle that's as true today as it was in olden days . . .

The prophet Daniel was greatly beloved of God. As a captured Israelite who was enslaved in Babylon, he so impressed his captors that he was eventually elevated to the equivalent position of prime minister under four different rulers in three different empires.[8] In the midst of an idolatrous and very wicked regime, his faithfulness in prayer to the one, true, living God was legendary. As a direct punishment for his faithfulness to God, Daniel was thrown into a den of hungry lions. Yet glory followed when God miraculously closed the mouths of the lions and King Darius, stunned by what happened, professed faith in the one, true, living God.[9]

And it's a principle that is true in present times . . .

Miss Audrey Wetherell Johnson was a woman greatly beloved of God. Born in England, educated in Europe, delivered from agnosticism, and transformed by God's grace into a gifted Bible teacher and preacher, she answered God's call to the mission field in China during the 1930s. After years of teaching pastors and church leaders in a theological seminary in Beijing, Miss Johnson was scooped up with other missionaries and placed in a Japanese concentration camp for three years of intolerable and unmentionable suffering. Yet once again we glimpse God's glory when we learn that Miss Johnson was finally released, came to America, and began Bible Study Fellowship, an international ministry that now has approximately one million men and women who use her material and format to study God's Word each week.

In the midst of our suffering, it can often be difficult to glimpse the glory to come. Suffering is so immediate and can seem so permanent that we can easily lose sight of the big picture. The pain can be so crushing and our hearts can be so broken that we just don't understand why! *Why me?* Whenever that question tends to fill my mind, I hear Him whisper to my heart, "Anne, why *not* you? Just trust Me!"

When I don't understand why, I trust Him because . . .

God loves even me!

Why Is God Silent?

Trusting God's Goodness

I do not ask my cross to understand
My way to see —
Better in darkness
just to feel Thy hand,
And follow Thee.

The family in Bethany must have been very confused by God's initial response to their prayers, because He was silent and still. He didn't do anything, and He didn't say anything. *Why?*

From the very beginning, God's ways have not been our ways, and God's thoughts have not been our thoughts. There is a mystery to God that can never be explained. Someone has said that if God were small enough for us to understand, He would not be big enough to save us. Yet the Bible is God's revelation of Himself to us. And the revelation is true . . .

At the birth of time and space and human history, against the inky blackness of the universe and the shadowy mysteriousness of eternity, the character of God shone forth with the radiant beauty of a full moon in a cloudless night sky. Even the casual reader of the creation account in Genesis can easily identify . . .

His unequaled power as He called into existence that which had no existence,

His unfathomable wisdom as He gave purpose and meaning to each aspect of His creation,

His unlimited sovereignty as He took counsel with Himself and decided to create man in His own image,

and His unsearchable goodness that was revealed when He created Adam, the first man.

God formed Adam with gentle, compassionate, skillful hands, giving him His own breath for life. His goodness permeated His preparation of a place for Adam to live as He made all the arrangements for Adam's comfort as well as enjoyment. Then He understood and satisfied the deep, lonely longing of Adam's heart by giving him Eve as his life's companion.

It was Eve who was the first person to be tempted to rebel against God, and one aspect of that fateful temptation was to doubt God's goodness to her. As she walked through her garden home one day, perhaps enjoying the tranquil perfection of the views around her as well as the satisfaction that was hers in being ruler over all, she felt the dew on the soft moss beneath her feet, smelled the fresh air that now and then carried with it the rich, heavy scent of blossoms, and felt the warmth of the sun on her skin. Eve, newly created, with the body of a woman yet the pure innocence and naiveté of a baby, was totally relaxed when she was approached by what was possibly the most magnificent of all the created animals. The serpent was also the smartest. He had planned his approach carefully, making contact with Eve when she was off guard and alone. The Genesis account says, "Now the serpent was more crafty than any of the wild animals the LORD God had made. He said to the woman, 'Did God really say, "You must not eat from any tree in the garden"?' "[1] Eve's lack of surprise when the serpent spoke to her indicates she was either so naive she didn't know that animals don't speak, or in the beginning, they did communicate in some way. In this case, Satan spoke through the serpent. And Eve, without warning, was face to face with temptation that included not only disobedience to God's Word but denial of God's goodness.

Dr. Larry Crabb, a prominent psychologist, defines sin as "our effort to supplement what we think are limits to God's goodness. It is trusting our self instead of trusting God."[2] Satan led Eve into thinking that God was holding out on her. He persuasively argued, "God knows that when you eat of it your eyes will be opened, and you will be like God, knowing good and evil."[3] In other words, "Eve, God knows this fruit is really good. But He's mean and doesn't want you to have it. Besides, He's also jealous and keeps all the best stuff for Himself."

Who is trying to convince you that God is not good? That your heavenly Father does not have your best interests in mind? That He is holding out on you in some way? Can you hear the hiss of the serpent in such reasoning?

Perhaps we are never more vulnerable to this temptation than when our hearts are broken and we cry out to God only to have Him remain silent. And in the silence, if we listen carefully, we will hear the hiss of that old serpent, "*If* God really does care, why doesn't He *do* something about your suffering? Why doesn't He at least *say* something? Maybe He's just got a cruel, capricious streak. We all do, you know. Or is He on vacation and unaware of what's going on? Or maybe He knows, but He's just indifferent. Or maybe He's not indifferent, just busy — and you are not high on His priority list. When you need Him, where is God?"

When have you cried out . . .

Lord, I'm hurting.
Lord, my loved one is hurting.
Lord, the one whom You love is sick.
Lord, my brother is sick in sin.
Lord, my friend is dying without You.
Lord, my heart is broken.
Lord, help me! Now! Please!

How has Jesus responded? Has He remained silent in your life? Has His lack of response caused you to doubt His goodness?

When Mary and Martha begged Jesus to help their brother, Lazarus, their sense of helplessness was reinforced because, not only had something bad happened to their brother, but when it did Jesus didn't respond to their plea. He must have seemed hidden . . .

out of touch . . .
uncaring . . .
remote . . .
removed.

Actually, Jesus *had* gotten their message. "Yet when he heard that Lazarus was sick, he stayed where he was two more days" (11:6). Jesus had heard, but *He did nothing about it.* Does that mean Jesus was aloof to their needs? Deaf to their plea? That He's just *not good?*

Who is your Lazarus? Who do you know who is not just physically sick but sick in his or her sin? Someone perhaps who has lost the appetite for kindness, truthfulness, righteousness, holiness, goodness, and responsibility? Someone who has lost the appetite for Jesus? Someone who is therefore growing weak morally and spiritually, becoming depressed and discouraged? Is your Lazarus your brother? Or sister? Or parent? Or spouse? Or child? Or in-law? Or friend? Has your prayer for your Lazarus remained unanswered? Does God seem to be hiding Himself from you?

Then be encouraged as you consider what Jesus did for Martha and Mary in answer to their plea on behalf of their brother! God's silence is never due to . . .
deafness
or indifference
or preoccupation with other things
or inability to act
or meanness.

God cannot be less than Himself, and God is good. His silence is not denial. Martha would discover that Jesus' silence was a purposeful delay. But this discovery was not immediate. It stretched out over at least a four-day period that must have seemed an eternity to the sisters' grief-stricken minds and broken hearts. But it was during the delay that their faith was stretched until they learned to trust God beyond the grave!

When I don't understand why, I trust Him because . . .

*God's silence can
deepen my faith in Him.*

Why Did God Let the Worst Happen?

Trusting God Beyond the Grave

I consider that our present sufferings
are not worth comparing
with the glory
that will be revealed in us.

— ROMANS 8:18

Have you ever specifically prayed for something only to have the prayer go unanswered and the situation get dramatically *worse?*

Have you ever prayed for your mother's health to improve only to have her condition weaken then deteriorate further when she had a negative reaction to the medication she was given?

Have you ever prayed for your job to be more productive only to lose out on a promotion and then receive notice that you were being fired from the company?

Have you ever prayed for your child's well-being only to have him or her drop out of school then be injured in a tragic car accident or become addicted to drugs?

Why?

Martha and Mary sent an earnest, hopeful message to Jesus about their brother, Lazarus: "Lord, the one you love is sick" (11:3). If they could have heard Jesus' response at the moment He received their plea, they initially might have been encouraged, because "when he heard this, Jesus said, 'This sickness will not end in death. No, it is for God's glory so that God's Son may be glorified through it'" (11:4). Hearing this response, the logical assumption would have been that Jesus knew God would not let Lazarus's illness become worse . . . that Lazarus would not die . . . that God would heal him.

When have you prayed and received initial encouragement through a promise from God? Has that promise added to your miserable confusion when, not only does it seem to be unfulfilled, but the very opposite happens?

As other Christian parents have done, I have prayed without ceasing for my children throughout the years. One of the promises I believe God gave me for them, and a promise I have claimed again and again in prayer, is Exodus 15:1–2. This passage is the song of Moses as he exults in God's deliverance of the Hebrew children when the Red Sea was parted and they crossed over on dry ground. As Pharaoh's army pursued and sought to keep God's children from getting safely to the Promised Land of His blessing, the sea's walls collapsed, the enemy was supernaturally destroyed, and God's people rejoiced:

I will sing to the LORD,
  for he is highly exalted.
The horse and its rider
  he has hurled into the sea.
The LORD is my strength and my song;
  he has become my salvation.
He is my God, and I will praise him,
  my father's God, and I will exalt him.

The promise God seemed to give me from this ancient hymn of joy was that He would supernaturally overthrow anything or anyone seeking to hinder my children from being in His place of blessing for their lives. I believed that God would be our strength and song and salvation as a family so that together we could exalt Him!

Then cancer struck my son. And hurricanes struck our property. And fire struck my husband's office. And the devil himself struck vital family relationships. Staggering from one disaster to the next, I felt the sea walls collapsing, not on the "army" that was pursuing me, but on *me!* In fact, in some areas, my head is not above water yet!

Why? Why does God let things go from bad to worse for those He loves — those like *me?* Like Martha and Mary?

Yet, consider this: When Jesus expressed words of encouragement concerning Lazarus's condition, Lazarus had already died![1] Was Jesus *lying?* Was His promise some sort of empty *"hope so"?* Was He just *toying* with Martha's and Mary's feelings? **NO!** What Jesus said meant . . .

that Lazarus's sickness did not have physical death as its ultimate purpose.

that God has a greater purpose than our immediate comfort.

that getting what we want, when we want it, is not always the best for us or glorifying to God.

For Mary and Martha, the greater purpose was to bring them to a point of absolute helplessness and hopelessness . . .

so that they might keep their focus on Him,

so that they might put all their faith in Him alone,

so that they might soar on eagles' wings,

so that they might bring glory to God . . .

as their faith gave Him opportunity to demonstrate in a spectacular, unmistakable way that His power and grace were totally sufficient for their need! Their faith gave Him the platform to prove by His actions that His claims of being the unique and only Son of God, of being the long-awaited Messiah, of being the Resurrection and the Life, were true!

Jesus was teaching Mary and Martha to trust Him . . .

beyond today,
beyond the physical,
beyond the emotional,
beyond the temporary,
beyond the material,
beyond the visible,
beyond the grave!

Trust Him when you can't see the big picture or the end of the story. Trust Him when the worst happens and you just don't understand why.

When I don't understand why, I trust Him because . . .

Even when my hopes are crushed, there is glory ahead.

Why Did God Do That?

Trusting God to Know Best

The LORD is my shepherd,
I shall lack nothing.
He makes me lie down
in green pastures,
he leads me beside quiet waters,
he restores my soul.
He guides me in paths
of righteousness
for his name's sake.
Even though I walk through the valley
of the shadow of death,
I will fear no evil,
for you are with me;
your rod and your staff,
they comfort me.
You prepare a table before me
in the presence of my enemies.
You anoint my head with oil;
my cup overflows.
Surely goodness and love
will follow me
all the days of my life,
and I will dwell in the house
of the LORD
forever.

— PSALM 23

Do you sometimes cry out, as I have, "God, don't You see my tears? Don't You see my broken heart? God, never mind me, but how can You bear to see the agony of my loved one? God, I know that You care. I just don't understand why You don't intervene in this situation right now. Why don't You do something? And, God, why did You do *that?*"

Then, to my heart, I seem to hear His still, small voice whispering, "Anne, trust Me. I know what's best." And I'm left to wonder why I think I know better than God what's best for me or my loved one. Mary and Martha had a lot to learn — like me.

The kind of trust God wants us to have cannot be learned in comfort and ease.

Mary and Martha could not learn it immediately or quickly. It required time. And patience. And suffering. And the pressure of desperation. Which is why, when Jesus "heard that Lazarus was sick, he stayed where he was two more days" (11:6). Jesus deliberately delayed answering the sisters' plea! They could not know *then* why Jesus did that. But we know now.

Several years ago I prayed earnestly for a relationship one of my children was in. As I continuously poured out my heart to God in tears and fasting and pleading, He remained silent. For months I could get no answer until finally I just collapsed in a spiritual heap and told Him I didn't know what to do; I was totally helpless. Then the situation got worse, so I began to argue with God. Every legitimate and imaginary fear I had ever thought came to the surface as, incredibly, *I warned Him* of the dire consequences that would follow if this relationship was allowed to progress. I told Him respectfully but in no uncertain terms what I thought He should do. All I can say from this perspective years later is that I praise God for His patience and sovereignty and unanswered prayers! Although my intense concern had been based on my discernment of the facts as I saw them at the time — and I believe my perception was accurate — what I lacked was the big picture. God knew that, by His grace, people and circumstances change and that the prayer of my heart would be answered, but in a totally different way than I had asked. I know through hindsight that He knows best!

Have you wondered, in agony, why God is doing what He's doing? Why He has delayed answering your prayer? Have you reacted to the delay by trying to help Him out and speed things up? Have you turned to . . .

a doctor,
a lawyer,
a counselor,
a friend,
a pop psychology,
a neighbor's sympathetic ear,
or
a popular TV talk show?

Have you resorted
to threats
or bargaining
or manipulation
until you're totally exhausted? Have you come to the absolute end of your rope?

One reason God may be delaying His answer to your prayer and postponing His intervention in your situation is to bring you to the end of your own resources. Sometimes God waits in order to allow us time to exhaust every other avenue of help until we finally realize without any doubt or reservation that we are totally helpless without Him.

Have you finally concluded that your situation is impossible and that if He doesn't help you, there will be no help? Have you finally reached the place where you have no one and no help — except Jesus? Then you may be close to experiencing the purpose for His delay, which may be to develop your faith in Him, and Him alone.

When Jesus did decide to respond to Mary and Martha's plea, His disciples thought the timing was all wrong, and they questioned His wisdom. After delaying for two days, Jesus told them, "Let us go back to Judea" (11:7). However, His disciples resisted, protesting, "But Rabbi . . . a short while ago the Jews tried to stone you, and yet you are going back there?" (11:8).

The disciples were arguing with Jesus!

Have *you* ever argued with Jesus? Have you ever questioned His wisdom or timing and honestly blurted out that what He seemed to be doing was not a good idea . . . not a good time . . . not the way to do things . . . in your opinion? It's amazing how arrogant we can be, isn't it?

Yet there are times when Jesus seems so slow to answer our prayers! And when He does begin to move into a situation, things can be so different from what we envisioned that we resist the answer we've been waiting for! Not only His *delays* but His *ways* can be totally confusing!

For generations, God's people have struggled to understand His ways. In ancient Judah, Habakkuk cried out for God to do something about the sin in his nation: "How long, O LORD, must I call for help, but you do not listen? . . . Why do you make me look at injustice? Why do you tolerate wrong?"[1] When God finally answered Habakkuk's plea, He revealed that He would use the Babylonians as His instrument of judgment on Judah. A horrified Habakkuk exclaimed, in essence, "O God, not that! Don't do *that!*"[2]

God's ways must have seemed incredibly confusing, not only to the disciples and to Habakkuk, but also to another Bible character who must have struggled to understand — but obeyed anyway. When Joshua went out on a military reconnaissance mission to assess Jericho, the enemy's mightiest stronghold, he was confronted by the

Commander of God's army, the preincarnate Son of God. The Commander instructed Joshua to take off his shoes because he was on holy ground in the presence of God. Joshua immediately obeyed. Then God surely gave Joshua the strangest strategy for overcoming Jericho that any general has ever been given! God told him to lead his armed men in a silent march around the outside walls of the city once a day for six days. On the seventh day, they were to march around the city seven times. On the last lap, the priests in the army were to blow trumpets loudly and the people were to shout. Then the wall would collapse, and Joshua's army could successfully capture the city!

I would love to have heard what all the retired generals supplying color commentary for the national television news would have said about *that* Operation Liberation! If I had been Joshua and received instructions like that, I think I would have asked God to give me His plan B — just in case the first plan didn't work! But Joshua did exactly as he was commanded, and on the seventh day, after the seventh lap, when the trumpets blew and the people shouted, the walls came down! And Joshua led his people in a great victory — and an answer to their prayers![3]

Like Joshua, Gideon was another leader of God's people who was given a confusing answer to his plea for help. He was confronted with an invading army of Midianites that was so huge it looked like grasshoppers stretching out along the plain as far as the eye could see. He mustered every fighting man he could find into an army of thirty-two thousand men. But God weeded out Gideon's army until only three hundred were left! Then God commanded Gideon to take the three hundred men and position them on the ridges surrounding the enemy encampment. Each man was to hold a flaming torch inside a clay water jar with one hand and a trumpet in the other hand. When Gideon gave the signal, the men were simultaneously commanded to break the water jars, lift high the torches, and blow the trumpets! Can you imagine Gideon's consternation over such instructions? But he obeyed! And the enemy fled, killing each other as they ran, giving Gideon a great victory — and an answer to his prayer![4]

God answers prayer, but sometimes the way He goes about it can be incredibly confusing and unconventional. Which is one reason He goes about it in that way —

so that our faith rests totally in Him. Then, when the answer comes, we know without a shred of doubt that it comes from Him alone and that He knows best. And we give Him all the glory.

Jesus knew Mary and Martha's anxious request would be answered, but in a totally different way than they had asked. And Jesus knew much better than His disciples what awaited Him this time in nearby Jerusalem, yet it was for this very time that He had been born. So He addressed their concerns by explaining, "Are there not twelve hours of daylight? A man who walks by day will not stumble, for he sees by this world's light. It is when he walks by night that he stumbles, for he has no light" (11:9–10). In other words, "Our life span is like a twelve-hour day. The length is predetermined and fixed. Just as we can't make the sun set one hour earlier, when we are in God's will we cannot shorten or lengthen our lives from what God has predetermined they should be. The important factor is to walk in the daylight of God's will, because then you will be safe; you will not stumble. If, on the other hand, you walk in the darkness outside of God's will, you remove yourself from His protection and subject yourself to everything and anything that comes along. And that's a dangerous place to be. It is God's will that I go to Jerusalem. Therefore, I will be safer there in the midst of the murderous, plotting enemy than I would be staying here in the tranquillity of the Transjordan outside of His will."

This principle came forcefully to my mind one morning when I was in Madras, India. I had been speaking at a conference of five thousand pastors and evangelists from every province in the country. One morning, before I went to the scheduled meeting, my traveling companion came rushing into the room, waving a long stream of paper. I recognized it as the news information that was disgorged by the Teletype machine in the lobby for English-speaking people who were interested in what was going on in the rest of the world. Across the paper, in two-inch-tall black letters, was the headline, "The War Has Begun!" As our eyes devoured the text, we learned that the United States had actually begun the war in the Persian Gulf to evict Saddam Hussein's army from the oil fields of Kuwait and liberate the tiny kingdom from his tyrannical grip.

As my companion and I looked at each other, we were acutely aware of the distance between us and the safety of our country. We were literally on the other side of the world in a nation that was not all that sympathetic to the action America had just taken. And we were two women, traveling alone. For all we knew, the entire world would be launched into war. It was then that Jesus' words to His disciples came clearly to mind. I was confident that my trip to India and my participation in the conference on evangelism was in God's will. Peace flooded my heart. I knew that I was safer on that platform in Madras during the first Persian Gulf War than I would have been at home. So I began my address that morning by telling the thousands of pastors and evangelists who were packed underneath an outdoor tent — men who, I knew, faced grave danger as they presented the gospel in a predominantly Hindu culture — that the safest place we can be is in the center of God's will. Because when we are in God's will, He takes full responsibility for us. And although bad things may happen, we have the assurance that they are for our good and His glory.

After Jesus and His disciples had had a lively exchange on the difference being in God's will makes to our personal safety and security, He informed them, "Our friend Lazarus has fallen asleep; but I am going there to wake him up" (11:11). And the disciples, so much like you and me, totally misunderstood Him, arguing, " 'Lord, if he sleeps, he will get better.' Jesus had been speaking of his death, but his disciples thought he meant natural sleep" (11:12–13).[5]

When have you totally misunderstood God's Word?

> *When He said,* "Love one another,"
>> did you think He meant for you to tolerate sin?[6]
>
> *When He said,* "Do not judge, or you too will be judged,"
>> did you think He meant for you not to take a stand against unrighteous behavior?[7]
>
> *When He said,* "In all things God works for the good,"
>> did you think He meant every story would have a happy ending?[8]
>
> *When He said,* "I will surely bless you,"
>> did you think He meant that He would make you healthy, wealthy, happy, and problem free?[9]

Isn't it amazing how we can misinterpret what He says?

I shared previously with you the promise from Exodus that I claimed for my children. When Moses remembered how God had hurled Pharaoh and his army into the sea, I understood God to mean that He would supernaturally overthrow anyone or anything that would hinder my children from being in the place of His blessing. But I interpreted that as meaning my children would be safe from those who would harm them. In actual fact, what He was really saying was that He would see to it that my children would be secure in His place of blessing. But I have discovered He sometimes allows them to have a frightening, traumatic Red Sea experience of pursuit and danger in the process.

Listening carefully is important, because if we misunderstand what God is saying, we set ourselves up for disappointment, discouragement, and disillusionment. We end up blaming God, becoming offended with Him when He doesn't keep the promise or fulfill His Word *as we understood it.* Had the disciples remembered this brief dialogue a short time later, they might have been spared three days of agony. Because Jesus *did* go to Jerusalem, He *was crucified* — and the disciples thought *it was a tragic mistake.* For three days they were lost in hopeless grief and terrified horror because they just didn't understand why God would do *that!* But Sunday came! Then they understood it had not been a tragic mistake but the glorious will of God, Who always knows best! Because it was through the Cross and the Resurrection that God's purpose for the life of Jesus was fulfilled and our redemption was accomplished! For three days the disciples had totally missed the blessing of what God was doing because they didn't trust Him to know best.

When I don't understand why, I trust Him because . . .

God's children are always secure in His will.

Why Doesn't God Protect Those He Loves?

*Trusting God's Plan
to Be Bigger Than Mine*

Joy also in this —
that your sufferings,
your losses and your persecutions
shall make you a platform from which
the more vigorously
and with greater power
you shall witness to Christ Jesus.

— C. H. SPURGEON,
Morning and Evening

Not only would the disciples be thrown into turmoil when Jesus was arrested within a few days, but on that hot, dry, and dusty day in the Transjordan, their misunderstanding of His words about Lazarus were also causing them confusion. Surely with no twinkle in His eye or smile on His lips but with grave resolution, "he told them plainly, 'Lazarus is dead, and for your sake I am glad I was not there, so that you may believe. But let us go to him' " (11:14–15).

Jesus was glad? He was *glad* Lazarus had *died* without Him?! What does that mean? We know it doesn't mean He enjoyed knowing that Lazarus had died or that He enjoyed thinking about the family's grief and despair. We know He truly felt their pain, according to Isaiah, who gave us a glimpse into the heart of God when he revealed, "In all their distress he too was distressed."[1]

Jesus was teaching His disciples — and you and me — a life lesson. And what a life lesson it is! The lesson is this: *There is a greater miracle than physical healing!* It's the miracle of the Resurrection! Be encouraged!

Even if your prayer is not answered
> and your financial problems are not solved
> and your marriage is not reconciled
> and your loved one is not healed
> and your child is not found —

there is hope! Jesus was *glad* because He knew not only the joy that was coming but the leaping strides of faith His disciples, as well as Mary and Martha — *especially* Martha — would experience because of it. He was glad because He knew God would be glorified to a far greater extent by the death and resurrection of Lazarus than He would have been by Lazarus's healing and recovery from sickness. Jesus did not protect Lazarus and his family from suffering and death because God had a bigger plan than just the immediate relief from pain.

There is more to life . . .

than being healthy,
than being happy,
than being problem free,
than being comfortable,
than feeling good,
than getting what we want,
than being healed.

There is more to life even than *living!*

And the "more to life" is the development of our faith to the extent that our very lives display His glory! So Jesus is glad, not that we suffer, but that we have the opportunity to grow in our faith and display His glory, which is the fulfillment of the very purpose for our existence. So He does not protect those He loves from bad things happening but uses bad things to fulfill His greater plan.

The apostle Paul went through a period of intense suffering that he described as being impaled with a spike! He testified that three times he pleaded with God to remove the suffering, but his prayer was unanswered. When he must have cried out through clenched teeth, *"Why?"* God reassured him, "My grace is sufficient for you, for my power is made perfect in weakness." Paul's response indicates he caught sight of the big picture when he responded, "Therefore I will boast all the more gladly about my weaknesses, so that Christ's power may rest on me. That is why, for Christ's sake, I delight in weaknesses, in insults, in hardships, in persecutions, in difficulties. For when I am weak, then I am strong."[2]

The apostle Peter, facing gruesome torture and death by crucifixion, encouraged others who were struggling with unanswered prayers when he wrote, "In this you greatly rejoice, though now for a little while you may have had to suffer grief in all kinds of trials. These have come so that your faith — of greater worth than gold, which perishes even though refined by fire — may be proved genuine and may result in praise, glory and honor when Jesus Christ is revealed."[3]

What kinds of trials have caused you to "suffer grief"? Could it be God has given you a platform of suffering from which you can be a witness of His power and grace to those who are watching? Because . . .

if we always feel good,
and look good,
and lead a good life . . .
if our kids always behave,
and our boss is always pleased,
and our home is always orderly,
and our friends are always available,

and our bank account is always
      sufficient,
  and our car always starts,
and our body always feels good . . .
  if we are patient,
    and kind,
      and thoughtful,
        and happy,
          and loving,
others *shrug* — because they're capable of
being that way, too, when everything goes
right.
  On the other hand . . .
          if we have a splitting headache,
        the kids are screaming,
      the phone is ringing,
    the boss is yelling, and
  the supper is burning,
yet we are still patient,
              kind,
                thoughtful,
                  happy,
                    and loving . . .
the world sits up and takes notice. The world
knows that kind of behavior is not natural.
It's supernatural. And the glory of Jesus is
revealed in us!
  Peter went on to say, "Though you have
not seen him, you love him; and even
though you do not see him now, you be-

lieve in him and are filled with an inexpressible and glorious joy, for you are receiving the goal of your faith."4 The goal of our faith is to glorify God. So while Jesus did not enjoy in the least seeing Martha suffer — in fact, He wept — He was glad that she was in the process of achieving the goal of her faith. His focus was on the big picture and the purpose of God that would be accomplished and the glory of God that would be revealed.

So often our primary ambition is to escape pain or feel good or be delivered from a problem when instead we need to keep our focus on the big picture of what God is doing in our life and the lives of others through pain or problems. Our primary aim should be to glorify God, not to be honored or to be healthy or to be happy.

This trust in God to accomplish His primary purpose is eloquently expressed by the widow of Todd Beamer. Todd was a passenger on the fateful United flight 93 when it was hijacked by suicide bombers on September 11, 2001. He and other passengers overpowered the hijackers, thwarting their use of the plane as a flying missile apparently aimed at the very heart of Washington, D.C. But the passengers were unable to prevent the plane from a nosedive crash into a vacant field in Pennsylvania, so September 11, 2001, was the date of Todd Beamer's entrance into heaven. Lisa Beamer gave us a snapshot of her faith that is being developed through suffering when she told an interviewer, "God says, 'I knew on September 10, and I could have stopped it, but I have a plan for greater good than you can ever imagine.' I don't know God's plan, and, honestly, right now I don't like it very much. But I trust that He is true to His promise in Romans 8:28."[5]

Thank you, Lisa, for trusting God when you don't understand why!

The disciples did not understand why Jesus had decided to go to Jerusalem at such a dangerous time. So, as He started out along the hot, dry, dusty road that would take Him to Bethany, did He walk alone? Did His disciples just sit there, staring at His back as He departed, totally confused by what all of this meant? Finally, Thomas, in a flat voice of discouraged resignation, "said to the rest of the disciples, 'Let us also go, that we may die with him' " (11:16).

As Thomas rose from where he had been sitting, his feet must have felt leaden. The timing of this whole thing seemed wrong to him. His entire demeanor was surely tinged with hopelessness. That hopelessness also pervaded the atmosphere in Bethany as the grief-filled tears of family and friends clouded their vision of God's greater purpose and His perfect timing in achieving it. Yet within twenty-four hours Thomas and the people of Bethany would have had emblazoned on their hearts and minds forever the amazing, unchangeable truth that God's plan is bigger than ours . . . and we can trust Him!

When I don't understand why, I trust Him because . . .

God has far greater miracles in mind than I could ever imagine.

Why Hasn't God Answered My Prayer?

Trusting God to Keep His Word

How long, O LORD?
Will you forget me forever?
How long will you
hide your face from me?
How long must I wrestle with my
thoughts
and every day have sorrow in my
heart?
How long will my enemy triumph over
me?

Look on me and answer, O LORD my
God.
Give light to my eyes, or I will sleep in
death;
my enemy will say, "I have overcome
him,"
and my foes will rejoice when I fall.

But I trust in your unfailing love;
my heart rejoices in your salvation.
I will sing to the LORD,
for he has been good to me.

— PSALM 13

After walking all day on rocky roads and over hills turned brown by the heat, Jesus and His disciples came to the little village He had come to love. As soon as He drew near, word spread quickly through all the "many Jews [who] had come to Martha and Mary to comfort them in the loss of their brother" (11:19). The sisters must have received the news at the same time together. Jesus had come! But Mary's obvious resentment that He hadn't answered their plea sooner and her hopeless despair over her brother's death kept her at home while Martha "went out to meet him" (11:20).

Did Martha run to Jesus, fling her arms around Him, sob on His shoulder, and pour out her heart? Or did she walk quickly from the house, weaving her way through her friends, until, with a more deliberate pace, she stood before Him? Was there a hurt, bewildered, accusing light in her eyes as she confronted Him, saying, "Lord, . . . if you had been here, my brother would not have died" (11:21)?

Have your thoughts been similar to Martha's?

God, where have You been?

Don't You know what we've been going through? Why haven't You answered sooner?

Why didn't You intervene? You could have prevented this tragedy.

Why didn't You come when we called? I thought You loved us.

Why did You let this happen?

Why didn't You answer my prayer?

I just don't understand.

Was Martha overlooking the fact that Jesus had drawn near to her in the midst of her suffering? He was present in her life, yet she was not comforted because she was so offended that He hadn't answered her the way she had wanted Him to.

Are you overlooking the fact that Jesus has drawn near to you?

Are you blinded to His presence by your own tears?

Are you deafened to His gentle voice by your own accusations?

Are you insensitive to His touch by your own withdrawal?

While God doesn't always protect those He loves from suffering or answer our prayers the way we ask Him to, He does promise in His Word that He will be present with us in the midst of our suffering and pain. He said, "Fear not, for I have redeemed you; I have called you by name; you are mine. When you pass through the waters, I will be with you; and when you pass through the rivers, they will not sweep over you. When you walk through the fire, you will not be burned; the flames will not set you ablaze. For I am the LORD, your God, . . . your Savior; . . . you are precious and honored in my sight, and . . . I love you."[1]

One of the most dramatic examples of God's presence in the midst of the suffering of those He loves is found in the Old Testament Book of Daniel. Daniel relates the story of three young men who were captured, dragged eight hundred miles from home, and stripped of their names and their manhood as they were enslaved to an emperor so cruel, sadistic, and absolute in his power that Saddam Hussein said he wanted to emulate him. Surely the three Hebrew teenagers were terrified as they went to sleep every night and woke up every morning desperate to know where God was! I wonder how often the three young teenage men from Jerusalem prayed, begging God to deliver them from the evil emperor Nebuchadnezzar's grip. But God didn't answer their prayers.

And then things got worse! The emperor built a huge golden statue of himself and demanded that everyone in his empire bow down in worship before it. When the Hebrews refused to obey, they were threatened with being burned alive in a furnace. Their answer to the cruel and unreasonable threat on their lives is a classic expression of sheer faith; they boldly stated, "If we are thrown into the blazing furnace, the God we serve is able to save us from it, and he will rescue us from your hand, O king. But even if he does not, we want you to know, O king, that we will not serve your gods or worship the image of gold you have set up."[2]

The fury of the king was as blazing as the furnace into which he tossed the three brave boys. The fire was so hot that the guards who threw them into the fire were themselves consumed by it. As King

Nebuchadnezzar looked intently into the furnace to see the charred remains of the three Hebrews, to his utter consternation he saw *four* men in the furnace! Walking about! Unsinged! He turned to his advisers and exclaimed, "Wasn't it three men that we tied up and threw into the fire? . . . Look! I see *four* men walking around in the fire, unbound and unharmed, and the fourth looks like a son of the gods."[3] The fourth man in that furnace was the preincarnate Son of God, drawing near to share in the suffering of those He loved. Jesus was with His children in the furnace!

The apostle John, suffering in exile on Patmos near the end of his life, must have prayed earnestly to be restored to his church and to his ministry. He must have begged God to get him off of the remote island so he could continue preaching and serving as a pastor and evangelist. Yet God didn't answer his prayers. Instead, John related that it was on Patmos that God drew near to him and gave him a vision of the glory of Jesus Christ — a vision he recorded for the encouragement of every generation of believers since that time in the Book of Revelation. Jesus was with him in exile on Patmos!

What is your fiery furnace of affliction?

Is it a leadership position where you are bombarded with criticism? Is it a physical body crushed in an accident or imprisoned in an illness that envelops you in agony? Is it your family that taunts and persecutes you because of Jesus' presence in your life?

What is your Patmos? A place where you are seemingly cut off and exiled from ministry and family? Is it a hospital bed? Or a small home with small children? Is it a workplace where you are surrounded by politically correct hostility to Christ? Is it another city or country you are forced to live in because of your marriage or job situation?

Then look up! God is with you! He promises to be with those who are in the fiery furnace or exiled on Patmos! Even if your suffering leads to death, He is with you! In Psalm 23, King David clung to the promise of God's presence when he wrote, "Even though I walk through the valley of the shadow of death, I will fear no evil, for you are with me."4

God draws near to those who are suffering at present, just as He drew near to those who suffered in the past . . . like the three Hebrew teenagers . . . like John . . . like King David . . . like Martha . . .

As Martha looked into the attentive,

tender face of Jesus, her heart must have softened. The resentment melted, and a ray of hope pierced through the blackness of her grief. She seemed to have been struck with sudden, startling insight: If this Man could create sight in a man born blind, if He could make the lame walk, if He could feed five thousand people with five loaves and two fish, *why couldn't He . . . ?* And so she put forth a tiny tendril of faith: "But I know that even now God will give you whatever you ask" (11:22).

I wonder if she took a deep breath and held it as she waited for His response. If so, she didn't have to wait long for it this time. He immediately answered by confirming her hope, revealing to her His intentions: "Your brother will rise again" (11:23). Martha's brow must have arched, then creased into a frown as she struggled to understand His meaning. "I know he will rise again in the resurrection at the last day," she answered (11:24). Is that where your faith is at the present time? "Lord, I know You can do that because the Bible says You will do it one day. But I doubt You will do it for me *now*." Do you believe intellectually, based on what the Bible says, that God has the power to answer your prayer, but you lack the personal faith to believe He will exercise it on your behalf now? Do you believe He has the power to act on your behalf tomorrow, but not today?

Jesus wanted to impress on Martha's heart and mind that she already had His power in her life. It was there, within her grasp. But that power would be *activated* by her faith. So He patiently persisted in developing Martha's faith until her focus was on Him, and Him alone. With eyes that must have seemed to penetrate past her doubting mind into her bleeding heart to the very depths of her being, He replied with words that have resonated through the centuries, giving hope at the gravesides of thousands of believers of every generation: "I am the resurrection and the life. He who believes in me will live, even though he dies; and whoever lives and believes in me will never die. Do you believe this?" (11:25–26).

Do *you* believe this? Do you believe
   that . . .
     when there is no hope,
      when there is no recourse,
       when there is no answer,
        when there is no help,
         when there is no way,
        when there is no remedy,
       when there is no solution,

when there is nobody,
that there *is hope* if you have Jesus? Do you believe that Jesus can make a way when there is no way?

Gradually, the light pierced through the depths of Martha's grief and despair, and she affirmed with a beautiful confession of faith, "Yes, Lord, . . . I believe that you are the Christ, the Son of God, who was to come into the world" (11:27). Martha recognized and acknowledged that apart from Jesus she was totally helpless and totally hopeless but that with Jesus, all things were possible — even resurrection from the dead!

Jesus had shifted Martha's focus from her own . . .

suffering
and grief
and pain
and problems
and despair
and hopelessness
and helplessness
to Himself.

Where is your focus? If you are suffering, is your focus on the pain? Or on the problems the pain produces? Or on the people who don't seem to understand or help as you think they should? As long as your focus is anywhere other than Jesus alone, you're going to feel defeated in helplessness and hopelessness.

But Jesus had also given Martha a promise on which she could hang her small thread of faith. He had promised her that her brother would rise again. He had promised her that "he who believes in me will live, even though he dies." Now He was challenging her to rest her faith in His Word.

On what have you hung your small tendril of faith as you have prayed for your loved one? Have you based your faith . . .

on a "hope so"?

on an earnest wish?

on an intense desire?

on a strong emotional feeling? . . .

as though, if you want it badly enough and can visualize it happening clearly enough, somehow it will come to pass? Have you based your faith . . .

on what someone else has told you God wants to do for you?

on what you have seen Him do for another person?

on what you think is fair or loving?

on what you think would be in the best interest of those involved?

on a doctor's recommendation for treatment?

You and I must pray in faith, or our prayer will not be pleasing to God.[5] If your faith as you pray is based on *anything other* than faith in God's specific promise given to you in His Word, then your prayer is on a shaky foundation. James, our Lord's half brother, who wrote a book with enormous practical application to daily Christian life, indicates that if your faith is not on a strong foundation you will very likely sooner or later be riddled with doubts, and your faith will be like the waves of the sea, "blown and tossed by the wind. That man should not think he will receive anything from the Lord."[6]

Are you discouraged because you have not received "anything from the Lord" as it relates to your prayer life? When Jesus' disciples were discouraged by their inability to get answers to prayer and so were ineffective in helping others, He encouraged them by pointing out that even faith the size of a mustard seed could move mountains.[7] The key to faith that works is the foundation on which it is placed.

Base your faith in prayer on God's Word. Ask Him to give you a promise that applies specifically to your situation. Then claim it persistently in prayer until God keeps His Word.

Are you unsure how to find a promise like that? I have been helped multiple times by a small volume of selected-and-combined Scripture passages entitled *Daily Light* that my family has used for generations. It was originally compiled by Jonathan Bagster of London, England, during his daily family devotions. My grandmother gave a volume to my mother when she was a young child in China. In fact, my mother can never remember a day of her life when she has not read it. My mother gave me my first volume on my tenth birthday. I have read it every day since. I gave a volume to each of my children as soon as he or she could read, and it has become a regular part of their daily devotions. To this day, one of the sweetest blessings is to know each morning and evening when I read *Daily Light* that my parents and children, wherever they might be, are reading the same thing.[8]

Without fail, the verses selected for a particular day's reading seem to specifically speak to that day's needs. In fact, God has spoken to me more often through the verses in *Daily Light* than through anything else. Again and again, He has given me answers to questions, direction for ministry, comfort in distress, wisdom for decisions, and promises to cling to from the various selected Scriptures. In my morning quiet time, I always begin by reading the Scripture selection in *Daily Light*. I then use those Scriptures as a basis for my prayers on behalf of others and myself.

One example of the blessing this has been and the way it has strengthened my faith in prayer at critical times is the way it seemed to speak to me on the morning of my son's surgery for cancer, March 6, 1998. Because the doctor surmised that Jonathan had had the cancer undetected for more than six years, the prognosis was very grim. As I got up early to go with Jonathan to the hospital for the surgery, I took the time to drop to my knees, opening my well-worn leather volume of *Daily Light*, searching for words of comfort or promises to claim. My tear-filled eyes fell on the following verses:

He . . . preserves the way of His saints. ✣ The steps of a good man are ordered by the LORD, and He delights in his way. Though he fall, he shall not be utterly cast down: for the LORD upholds him with his hand. ✣ Many are the afflictions of the righteous, but the LORD delivers him out of them all. ❦ . . . We know that all things work together for good to those who love God, to those who are the called according to His purpose. ❦ With us is the LORD our God, to help us and to fight our battles.

The LORD your God in your midst, the Mighty One, will save; He will rejoice over you with gladness.[9]

The peace that penetrated my heart as I claimed these promises for my son burst into hope and joy! The emotional nightmare I had been living dissipated *before* I even got to the hospital! I was able to be with Jonathan in total confidence that all was well. *And it was!* Because I knew that God would be with us regardless of the outcome, that all of Jonathan's circumstances would ultimately be for his own good and God's glory, and that God would be in our midst. I knew we could trust God to keep His Word.[10]

When I don't understand why, I trust Him because . . .

*God is intimately involved
in every area of my life.*

Why Didn't God Intervene?

Trusting God to Be on Time

Be assured that if God waits
longer than you could wish,
it is only to make the blessing
doubly precious.

— ANDREW MURRAY

Martha's small, mustard seed–sized faith was founded on Jesus and the promise He had given her. The hope that seemed to have been birthed in her spirit as a result of her faith caused her to go eagerly to Mary, drawing her aside privately to tell her, "The Teacher is here . . . and is asking for you" (11:28). Mary's broken heart must have shattered even more as the "if only's" flooded to the surface. Without thinking of the scene or commotion she would cause, she abruptly got up from where she had collapsed in the house and fled through the door.

"When the Jews who had been with Mary in the house, comforting her, noticed how quickly she got up and went out, they followed her, supposing she was going to the tomb to mourn there" (11:31). With almost frantic despair, as Mary ran through the narrow streets of the little village, did she stumble over the sharp stones? Did she cry afresh at the misery of her helplessness, hot tears blinding her eyes and streaming down her cheeks, disheveled hair escaping from underneath her veil and falling over her face? Finally, when she "reached the place where Jesus was and saw him, she fell at his feet and said, 'Lord, if you had been here, my brother would not have died' " (11:32).

Mary wasn't just being emotional. She was totally realistic. Her grief was coupled with a sense of total hopelessness and helplessness because death is so final. While someone has even a thread of life, there is hope. But once that person dies, there is no hope — no help at all. Although Mary's attitude was worshipful and respectful as she fell at Jesus' feet, she just couldn't quite manage to get beyond the despairing defeat of her brother's death. Any faith she might have had disintegrated as she lost her focus on Jesus and put it instead on herself and on her suffering and on the past and on what might have been, if only . . .

Are you haunted by the ghosts of *if only's* in your past?

"*If only* I hadn't gone there."

"*If only* I'd never met her."

"*If only* I had prayed about it."

"*If only* I had spent more time with him."

"*If only* I had stopped her."

"*If only* I had taken it seriously."

"*If only* I had known then what I know now."

"*If only* Jesus had answered my prayer when I had asked Him to."

"*If only* Jesus was here . . ."

If only's that are rooted in a sense of alienation and separation from God are cries of utter despair and hopelessness.

Thomas Merton, a solitary monk, expressed his alienation from God in an eloquent description of despair: "I sat there in the dark, unhappy room, unable to think, unable to move, with all the innumerable elements of my isolation crowding in upon me from every side: without a home, without a family, without a country, without a father, apparently without any friends, without any interior peace or confidence or light or understanding of my own — without God, too, without heaven, without grace, without anything!"[1]

In utter loneliness, having been separated from God during her time of need and now alienated from Him by her resentment, Mary was preoccupied with reliving those awful moments that had led to her brother's death, and all she could stammer was, "If you had been here . . ."

Mary thought Jesus was late. Do you think that now? Do you think He has shown up . . .

> too late to prevent the wedding,
> too late to prevent the pregnancy,
> too late to prevent the abortion,
> too late to prevent the accident,
> too late to prevent the rape,
> too late to prevent the death?

He's just too late!

Mary thought if He had truly understood their helpless situation He would have acted or answered differently. But as it was, she thought He was too late, and now she was not just helpless, she was totally, utterly hopeless.

Our questioning of God's timing struck me as I sat in a circle of people and listened as Chuck Colson, best-selling author and founder of Prison Fellowship, described his recent struggle with this same issue. He related that two years ago David Bloom, a television news commentator with the National Broadcasting Corporation, had given his heart to Christ while reading Chuck's book *Born Again*. Following his conversion, David had joined a weekly Bible study, where he seemed to soak up all he could learn. He was growing strong and deep in his new faith. Whenever Chuck was in New York, he would visit David for mutual encouragement.

As an increasingly prominent television commentator, David chose to go to Iraq during Operation Iraqi Freedom and was embedded with a military unit. The armored personnel carrier in which he traveled was nicknamed the "Bloom-mobile." One morning, as he was climbing out of the dusty vehicle in which he had been cramped for hours, he collapsed. He was rushed to a medical unit but was dead on arrival from a pulmonary embolism.

As Chuck told this story to our small circle, he transparently shared his reaction to the news of David Bloom's death: "*Why?* Why, God, did You let this happen? Finally we had an evangelical Christian in a strategic position within a major TV network! He was young and popular and extremely successful. *If only* You had saved his life! Why would You let him die such an untimely death when he could have served You so significantly with his life?"

A week later, Chuck attended David Bloom's memorial service at St. Patrick's Cathedral in downtown Manhattan. Leaders from the media; from city, state, and national governments; and from the television industry, as well as prominent citizens and entertainers, family, and friends, packed the service. Most who had come to pay their respects had no knowledge of David's faith in Jesus. But during the memorial, the e-mails he had written from Iraq to his wife, Melanie, were read. One after another, for the entire distinguished assembly to hear, those e-mails powerfully and poignantly described his faith in Jesus Christ. As Chuck Colson sat among the rows of mourners, he was struck by the realization, *God, now I understand one reason why! You've received so much glory in David's death!*

The last e-mail, which Melanie reportedly received from David just hours before his death, was published in a national magazine and bore this testimony:

You can't begin to fathom, cannot begin to even glimpse the enormity of

130

the changes I have and am continuing to undergo. God takes you to the depths of your being, until you're at rock bottom, and then, if you turn to Him with utter and blind faith and resolve in your heart and mind to walk only with Him and towards Him, picks you up with your bootstraps and leads you home.[2]

Home! The way by which God leads us home is often very different from what we imagine or desire or expect. For David, it was a dusty desert road. Yet the end of the road is the same for all of us who place our faith in Jesus. Because home is where He is. Home is heaven!

Since Chuck Colson shared his moving insights about David Bloom, I have prayed repeatedly for David's wife, Melanie, and their three daughters, Nicole, Ava, and Christine. Because while David's death brought glory to God . . . and while David is home in heaven . . . his family walked out of that cathedral without a father and without a husband to an empty house.

Why?

I am reminded that there is a mystery to God's timing that one day we will understand. And the life's lesson that Mary learned in Bethany so long ago is one that reassures us still today . . .

God is *never too late.*

He is *never too early.*

He is *always* right on time!

But . . . His timing can be very different from ours!

When I don't understand why, I trust Him because . . .

God is always on time for His purposes in my life.

Why Hasn't God Met My Needs?

Trusting God to Be Enough

Measure thy life by loss
and not by gain,
Not by the wine drunk,
but by the wine poured forth.
For love's strength standeth
in love's sacrifice,
And he who suffers most
has most to give.

Mary crumpled, sobbing, at the feet of Jesus. Oh, how she needed Jesus! But in the moment of her grief, she just didn't believe He was enough! She needed someone who understood the feelings of her grief. She needed someone who understood from personal, firsthand experience the agonizing despair and hopeless finality of death. She needed someone who understood her aching heart that was bruised and crushed under the weight of such irreplaceable loss.

As Mary lay with her shoulders shaking and her chest heaving, racked with pain that was too great to bear, the friends who had followed her voiced their own despair over her grief, and they wept too. The chorus of weeping was a symphony of sympathy. At the sight and sound of the poignant scene, Jesus "was deeply moved in spirit and troubled" (11:33). The text indicates He felt more than just grief; He felt anger.

Several years ago, I received an urgent call from a person who was at the local hospital, telling me that one of my dearest friends was dying. I couldn't believe what I was hearing. When I had spoken with the friend the day before, she had been healthy and happy. What could have gone so terribly wrong? As I rushed to the hospital, I kept praying, "Lord, help! The one whom we love is sick — dying!"

When I made my way into the hospital waiting room, I found her extended family huddled in tears and shock. I was told my precious friend had somehow breathed in a virus that had acted like a hand grenade in her body, exploding and destroying her internal organs. In grief and shock myself, I was urged to go into the chapel where her husband and children had gathered to pray. As I slipped into the darkened sanctuary and virtually collapsed onto a pew, I heard the whispered prayers and the sobs of her loved ones. Then the stifled grief erupted in a chilling, heart-wrenching cry as her son yelled out, "God, it's not right.

It's not right! It's just not right!"

Later, when her family made the decision to disconnect her from life support, and my beloved friend went to her heavenly home, her son's agonized, angry grief echoed in my ears, and I thought, *He was right. This is wrong. Terribly wrong! This was never meant to be.*

In the beginning, we were never intended to die. Death was not a part of God's original plan. He created you and me for Himself. He intended us to live with Him and enjoy Him forever in an uninterrupted, permanent, personal, love relationship. But sin came into our lives and broke the very relationship with God for which we were created. All of us are affected by this broken relationship because all of us are infected with sin.[1] Everyone who is born into the human race has sinned and fallen short of that original purpose of uninterrupted fellowship with God. And the consequence of sin is death — physical death and eternal death.[2] When a believer physically dies, even though he or she has received the gift of eternal life and therefore is saved from eternal death, and even though the believer is immediately ushered into the presence of the heavenly Father,[3] the pain and grief and separation inflicted on the loved ones left behind were never meant to be. It's as though sin and Satan have a temporary victory, even though the sting of death and the grave has been removed by the death and resurrection of Christ.[4]

When your loved one dies and your grief is tinged with anger, don't direct it toward God. He's angry too. Direct it toward sin and its devastating consequences. Dedicate yourself to sharing the gospel as often as you can. Pray that through your witness others who face physical death will choose to escape the second death, which is hell, the ultimate separation from God, by placing their faith in Jesus Christ.[5] As we face death, our only hope is in knowing there is genuine, triumphant, permanent victory over it that is available to us in Jesus' Name!

At my friend's funeral, I had the opportunity to address the hundreds gathered, and I shared with them that death is not right, but — thanks be to God! — because of His Son, Jesus, death is not final. When we place our faith in Him, not only will we go to heaven, but one day, in our flesh, we will see our loved ones again who have gone before us.[6]

That day in Bethany, as Mary wept and her friends wept with her, a tumult of grief and anger and compassion and empathy welled up within the heart of Jesus until He could no longer contain it. In a voice that must have been choking with emotion, He inquired, "Where have you laid him?"

Those around Him replied gently, "Come and see, Lord" (11:34).

When have you invited Jesus to "come and see"?

When have you prayed,

"Lord, come and see my pain . . . my hurt . . . my grief"?

"Come and see my broken heart . . . my broken hopes . . . my broken home"?

"Come and see my discouragement . . . my despair . . . my doubts"?

"Come and see the consequences of wrong choices . . . and failures . . . and sin"?

"Come and see my weakness . . . and fearfulness . . . and emptiness"?

"Come and see my guiltiness . . . and my sadness . . . and my loneliness"?

Have you erected a shield around your heart to prevent Him from seeing? A shield . . .

of pride
or doubt
or shame
or anger

or resentment
or busyness?
Did you think that if you opened your heart and let Him see inside, that He would blame you for what you have or haven't done? Or rebuke you for your lack of faith?

You and I can be so foolish! Why do we think we can hide our feelings from God? Why would we *want* to hide our feelings from God? Maybe it's due to the secret resentment of Him we harbor or the resistance to Him we feel because, after all, if He had been on time this never would have happened. How could He understand how we feel anyway?

There is no shield thick enough
or big enough
or strong enough
or tough enough
to hide us from His eyes of loving compassion. He sees right through the shield, just as He knew without asking exactly where the tomb was in Bethany and who was in it and how long he had been there and what the source of all the mourning and suffering was. He simply wanted those who were suffering to show Him what was wrong and tell Him how they felt.

Would you open up your heart and show it to Jesus? Show Him your grief and pain and let Him see exactly how you feel and what you think. Don't hide it or repress it or cover it up or pretend it's not there. Just pour it all out to Him, and then wait expectantly for His response.

When Jesus was invited by the mourners in Bethany to "come and see," *He wept!* (See 11:34–35.)

Jesus, the Creator of the universe, the eternal I Am, the Lord of life, knew He was going to raise Lazarus from the dead. Yet One so strong, so powerful, so wise, *so human,* stood there with tears running down His cheeks! *Why?* Because He loved those gathered at the tomb so much their grief was His.

When my youngest daughter, Rachel-Ruth, was small, she wore long braids as a means of controlling her naturally curly hair, which she hated. I will never forget an incident that followed the visit to our home of a beautiful young woman who had long, sleek, glossy brown hair. As soon as the door closed behind the young woman, Rachel-Ruth ran into the living room, jerking at her braids, tearing at her bangs, covering her face with her hands, and hysterically sobbing, "I hate my hair! My face is so ugly! I'm not pretty at all!"

Not knowing what had triggered this outburst, I just held her and wept with her. I looked up to see my other daughter, Morrow, standing in the doorway, weeping too. We wept because Rachel-Ruth was so distraught, and we loved her. Her torment was our own.

When was the last time you wept into your pillow at night, thinking no one cared? Is the pain so deep and your hurt so great that you cry night after night? In your misery and loneliness, do you think Jesus is emotionally detached? That He just doesn't care? Or that He's simply too busy to notice? Or that He is somewhat callous since He sees a lot of pain that's worse than yours? Or that *He* couldn't possibly understand how *you feel?* Or that *He's not enough* to meet your needs? Did you know that *Jesus weeps with you?* Did you know He puts all your tears in a bottle because they are precious to Him?[7] He has said in all of your afflictions, He Himself is afflicted.[8] Why? Because Jesus *does* understand! And *He loves you!*

Your suffering is His.

Your grief is His.

Your torment is His.

Your misery is His.

And He feels your pain!

He understands!

And He is enough to meet your needs!

Those who had gathered to support and comfort and help the family of Lazarus observed the famous young Rabbi weeping and concluded, "See how he loved him!" (11:36). Even though Jesus knew the glory to come, and the heavenly home that was being prepared, and the demonstration of God's power that was about to be displayed, Jesus wept! He wept for no other reason than He loved this precious family and they were weeping.[9] Jesus was entering into their suffering, even as one day He would ask us to enter into His at the Cross when we repent of our sin, die to ourselves, and receive Him by faith.

There were those in the crowd around Lazarus's tomb who refused to let go of their bitterness and resentment and offense with God because He had not answered their prayers as they thought He should. There were those who wallowed in self-pity and anger that God hadn't conformed to their schedule and given in to their demands. And so they snarled under their breath, "Could not he who opened the eyes of the blind man have kept this man from dying?" (11:37). Or, in other words, "If Jesus truly loved Lazarus, Mary, and Martha, He never would have let Lazarus die."

Is that what friends have said to you as they have sought to "comfort" you? Have they said that if God really loved you and your family, He would have intervened . . . He would have done things differently . . . He never would have let this bad thing happen?

Like your "comforters," some of the mourners in Bethany refused to understand that there is sometimes a greater purpose to suffering than being relieved of it. They were oblivious to the fact that there is sometimes a greater expression of love than giving the loved one everything he or she wants or demands. The mourners at Bethany had no inkling of how much Jesus did care and how deeply and personally He truly understood their suffering. They just clung to their own human understanding of the facts and believed the situation to be beyond anyone's ability to help. Because if a Man Who had created sight in one born blind could not even manage to come on time and save His friend from dying, there was nothing anyone could do. They knew at this stage, with Lazarus not only dead but in the tomb four days, *it would take a miracle . . .*

When I don't understand why, I trust Him because . . .

God understands my feelings.

Why Doesn't God Perform a Miracle?

Trusting God Alone

I pray also
that the eyes of your heart
may be enlightened
in order that you may know
the hope to which he has called you,
the riches of his glorious inheritance
in the saints,
and his incomparably great power
for us who believe.
That power is like the working
of his mighty strength,
which he exerted in Christ
when he raised him from the dead
and seated him at his right hand
in the heavenly realms,
far above all rule and authority,
power and dominion,
and every title that can be given,
not only in the present age
but also in the one to come.

— EPHESIANS 1:18–21

Do you believe in miracles? We know Jesus performed miracles, and we know miracles occurred with some frequency in the early church. But do they still happen today? Several years ago *Time* magazine ran a cover story about miracles that included the entire spectrum of opinion, from Cicero, who concluded pessimistically, "What was incapable of happening never happened, and what was capable of happening is not a miracle. . . . Consequently, there are no miracles," to Thomas Aquinas, who stated emphatically, "Christ was either liar, lunatic, or Lord," to Walt Whitman, who sentimentalized, "To me every hour of the light and dark is a miracle, every cubic inch of space is a miracle."

A miracle has been described as a "morsel of grace offered by a merciful God willing to meddle with the laws of His universe." Jesus called miracles "signs" to draw attention to the fact that miracles are not an end in themselves but a means to a greater end. They serve as signs directing us to a deeper, broader, more important truth that God is teaching.

" 'Touch me, heal me,' the crowds demanded of their Messiah, and so even as He went about touching and healing, He acknowledged that miracles, if produced on demand, could sabotage the faith they were meant to strengthen. For the truly faithful, no miracle is necessary; for those who must doubt, no miracle is sufficient."[1]

We seem the most desperate for a miracle when we are suffering either physically, emotionally, mentally, or relationally. Miracles spell relief and deliverance and escape and victory. The story of Lazarus includes perhaps the most magnificent miracle Jesus performed while here on earth. But the story of Lazarus is really the story of Martha's faith — and the necessity of placing our own faith in Jesus alone if we ourselves are to live life, not just somehow, but triumphantly . . . and if we are to experience the greatest miracle of all, that of passing from spiritual death to eternal life as we are born again into the family of God. In a larger sense, it's also the story of Martha's transition from faith to trust.

As Jesus made His way through the crowd outside the tomb, He ignored the curious stares and resentful glares of the bystanders. When He reached the tomb where Lazarus had been buried, with the blazing sun beating down on His head, "once more [He was] deeply moved" (11:38). Did He have the chilling thought and the deep foreboding and the nauseating dread of another death and another tomb to come? Was He thinking of other friends and family members and disciples who would be numbed with horror and helplessness and hopelessness as they looked on a similar grave that entombed the body of Another? Was He experiencing a flash-forward to *His own* death and burial?

Surrounded by a crowd of friends, family, and just curious onlookers, He gazed at the scene before Him. I expect Mary and Martha followed His focus that was fixed on the cave carved out of the hillside that served as Lazarus's burial place. A large stone sealed off the entrance to the tomb. Perhaps the fresh sight of it caused Mary to collapse in a renewed paroxysm of agonizing despair as she wept uncontrollably.

Regardless of Mary's condition, Martha was jolted out of any grief-filled reverie that preoccupied her thoughts when she heard His familiar voice command quietly but with absolute authority, "Take away the stone" (11:39). Nothing could have been more appalling to her! She cringed at the mere thought of such a thing. Her grief had been great but had been somewhat finalized by having her brother buried. To reopen his tomb seemed to serve no purpose except to reopen the fresh wound of her heart. How could Jesus say such a thing? *How could He even think such a thing?*

What stone is keeping your loved one buried in sin and spiritual death? Is it his or her own pride? Or unbelief? Has Jesus told *you* to roll it away? And is it unthinkable to you?

Jesus didn't tell Lazarus to roll away the stone; He told *Lazarus's sister Martha* to have the stone rolled away. He knew the stone had to be removed in order for Lazarus to be set free and for others to see the power and glory of God in his life.

What stone is Jesus commanding *you* to remove before He can work a miracle in the life . . .

of your brother
or your sister
or your husband
or your wife
or your child
or your parent
or your daughter-in-law
or your son-in-law
or any in-law
or your friend
or your neighbor
or your coworker
or your boss
or your pastor
or your church?

Would your brother experience the power of God in his life if you would remove the stone of rivalry?

Would your sister experience the power of God in her life if you would remove the stone of jealousy?

Would your husband experience the power of God in his life if you would remove the stone of a nagging tongue?

Would your wife experience the power of

God in her life if you would remove the stone of unkindness?

Would your parent experience the power of God in his or her life if you would remove the stone of unforgiveness?

Would your child experience the power of God in his or her life if you would remove the stone of favoritism?

Would your church experience the power of God in its life if you would remove the stone of hypocrisy?

Would your pastor experience the power of God in his life if you would remove the stone of criticism?

Would your boss experience the power of God in his life if you would remove the stone of laziness?

Would your neighbor experience the power of God in her life if you would remove the stone of prejudice?

Would our nation experience the power of God in its life if we would remove the stone of prayerlessness?

The stones are endless, aren't they? Piles and piles of stones are heaped over the entrance to the tombs of those around us who are dead and buried in sin. And this whole time, while we've been mourning their death, Jesus says to you and me, "If you want to see Me work in the life of your

Lazarus, take away the stone."

Could it be that one reason we have yet to see the outpouring of God's power and glory in our home and neighborhood and city and state and nation and world is because people like you and me refuse to be obedient?!

Martha, with what surely was a look of horrified indignation on her face, blurted out, "But, Lord, . . . by this time there is a bad odor, for he has been there four days" (11:39). Her immediate, impulsive response was typically practical. She knew that the heat of the days would have hastened the corruption of the body that had been lifeless long enough for decay to set in. And so, in effect, she argued, "But, God, he's been dead too long to be raised!"

Who do you think has been dead too long to be raised to newness of life? Do you have someone on your prayer list like that? Or have you dropped that person off your list and discarded him or her from your prayers because the person has been dead so long you've lost all hope that he or she could ever be raised?

While we should be removing the stones, we're arguing with Jesus about how ineffective such an effort is going to be! Or

we're telling Him . . .
how to answer our prayers and
how to solve our problems and
how to relieve our stress and
how to heal our hurts and
how to comfort our grief and
how to reconcile our marriage.
And Jesus is saying, "Don't tell Me what to do or how to do it. Just roll away the stone."

When Jesus is seeking to do a miracle in the life of your loved one, why do you argue with Him about His methods? What is your argument?

"If I submit, my husband will walk all over me."

"If I share the gospel, someone will ask me a question I can't answer."

"If I forgive that person, she will get by with what she has done to me."

"If I deny myself, take up my cross, and follow Christ, I'll never get what I want."

Maybe Martha resisted rolling away the stone because she was afraid of failure. What if she rolled it away and nothing happened? It would not only embarrass her but damage the credibility of Jesus in the eyes of her friends.

Are you embarrassed to lead family devotions? Teach Sunday school? Share your testimony? Witness to a neighbor? Are you afraid God somehow will not be sufficient if you step out in faith and obedience to His command?

Jesus stands ready to help us, but His help is contingent on our absolute, total obedience to His Word, whether or not we agree with it or understand it. His help is delayed and His power is bound and His glory is hidden as long as we stand around in disobedience and argue! Martha delayed her own joy as well as the work of God in her brother's life while she stood there and argued with her Lord.

"But, Lord, . . ." is an oxymoron, isn't it? It's a contradiction in terms, because if Jesus is Lord, then we say, "Yes, Sir," not, "But, Lord."

What glory and joy are you missing because you refuse to take away the stone? Stop arguing! Stop refusing! Take away the stone! How will you ever experience the power and the glory of God in your life or the life of someone else if you attempt only those things you are sure you can do? If you stay in your comfort zone?

Jesus turned His full gaze onto Martha with a look that surely melted her resistance and silenced her argument. With patient firmness, He challenged her not only to obedience but to expectant faith: "Did I not tell you that if you believed, you would see the glory of God?" (11:40). In essence, He was saying, "It's time to just trust Me. Place all of your small, mustard seed–sized faith in Me and My promise to you." And still today Jesus is telling us it's time to leave . . .

> low living
> and sight walking
> and small planning
> and smooth knees
> and colorless dreams
> and tame visions
> and mundane talking
> and cheap giving
> and dwarfed goals![2]

Jesus was telling Martha, as He tells us today, *"It's time to soar on eagles' wings!"*

When Jesus had revealed to Martha that He is "the resurrection and the life. He who believes in me will live, even though he dies" (11:25) then asked if she believed Him, she said she did. But "faith by itself, if it is not accompanied by action, is dead."[3] Martha had said she had faith. She intellectually believed what Jesus had said. But Martha needed to make the transition from faith to trust. Because while belief is

158

the consent of the mind and faith is a choice of the will, trust is a commitment of the heart.

The time had come for Martha to put her faith into action by surrendering all of her hopeful expectations and heartfelt longings and practical common sense and simply trust Him when she didn't understand. And her obedience to His word would be proof that her faith had made the eighteen-inch drop from her head to her heart.[4]

In some way, God requires more than our intellectual faith — He requires our total trust as demonstrated by our obedience to His Word in order to release the miracle. Jesus gave sight to a man born blind, but in order to receive it he had to trust and obey by going to the pool of Siloam to wash.[5] Jesus gave strength to a paralyzed man who had been lying on his pallet for thirty-eight years, but he had to trust and obey by getting up and picking up his mat before he could walk.[6] Jesus healed a man with a withered hand, but before it could be straightened, the man had to trust and obey by stretching it out.[7]

Again and again, during my years of ministry, I have observed those who are much more gifted at teaching than I am and who seem to long to exercise their gifts — yet never ardently pursue the opportunities they are given. Often they come up to me after I've delivered a message and inquire emphatically, "Anne, I want to do what you do and feel called to do it. How do I get where you are?" They say they feel called, but when it comes down to hard choices, they compromise their time by giving it to lesser pursuits, or squander their emotions on television or movies, or settle for a limited and consequently easier sacrifice. They talk about what they could do, they pray about what they could do, they even seek counsel from others about what they could do, but they *don't just do it!* They seem to have made a head-choice to believe but not a heart-commitment to trust. As a result, they will never experience the fullness of God's power at work in and through their lives to raise others from the spiritually dead!

I've seen that same attitude in various people who are constantly complaining about how overweight they are. These people think about dieting and talk about dieting and read about dieting, and some even dabble in dieting. But in my experience, dieting never works unless I want to lose weight more than I want to eat that forbidden food!

When it comes to experiencing God, I have to choose Him at all cost. I have to be willing to step out of the boat, as Peter did in Matthew 14, risking total failure in the eyes of others, in order to discover first-hand His power enabling me to walk on the water when He bids me, "Come." Again and again, I've been confronted with hard choices when I've had to throw caution to the wind and abandon myself to faith in Him, and Him alone . . .

> when I step into a pulpit,
> when I pick up my pen to write,
> when I hire a new staff person,
> when I establish a new aspect of our ministry,
> when I commit our ministry to much more than we have resources to underwrite.

Whenever I choose to step out in faith and trust Him, I'm actually choosing to take Him at His Word, put Him to the test, and *just do it!* The result is the thrilling adventure called the Christian life.

Something in Martha must have been quickened as she saw the intensity in the

Lord's eyes. She knew this was no longer the time to talk about it or pray about it or think about it. The spark of faith was suddenly fanned into flame, and without further question or word, *she just did it!* She ordered the stone to be rolled away. Simply because He said so. Her obedience, her dependence, and her expectance were in Him alone. He was all she had.

When have you been in a situation where you had nowhere to turn and no place to go and no one to help you? When have you been consciously aware that all you had was Jesus?

I am convinced that one reason Jesus allowed Martha to suffer was to bring her to the point of personal desperation so that she could discover the truth of that same simple yet profound, life-changing lesson and just trust Him when she didn't understand. As the stone was rolled away, the sound of weeping and mourning and whispering must have been hushed in startled amazement. Everyone had been staring at Jesus and Martha. Their conversation had been private. No one could have heard what had been said between them, especially since they were surrounded by the wailing and weeping of the mourners. Now, without any preliminaries, the crowd was suddenly aware that the stone to the tomb was being rolled away. In the heat of the day, there was total silence. There may have been the sound of grasshoppers whirring in the tall grass, or a bird calling its mate from the tree, or the rustling of a dried leaf as a breath of hot air blew it across the stones. But the silence must have been deafening.

I wonder if Martha was momentarily embarrassed when the stone was rolled away in front of all her friends. Because she knew that even if the assembled friends had been unable to see Lazarus in the darkened depths, they would have been able to smell him. There was no doubt that he was dead.

With every eye fastened on Him — the red-rimmed eyes of Mary, the hope-filled eyes of Martha, the grieving eyes of the friends, the hostile eyes of the unbelievers, the astonished eyes of the casual observer — Jesus boldly, loudly lifted His voice for all to hear as He prayed, "Father, I thank you that you have heard me. I knew that you always hear me, but I said this for the benefit of the people standing here, that they may believe that you sent me" (11:41–42). Jesus was letting everyone know that if Lazarus was raised, the power to make it happen came from God.[8]

Then . . .

> in the same Voice that had brought the world into being,
> the same Voice that had called Abraham from Ur,
> the same Voice that had reverberated from Mount Sinai,
> *that same Voice* thundered, "Lazarus, come out!" (11:43).[9]

The voice of the Creator was commanding into existence that which had no existence!

In the heavy silence that followed, the sound of His voice must have echoed from the stone walls and wafted on the gusting breeze while every eye must have strained toward the cave, peering into the black hole where the stone had been. How long did they have to wait before they saw movement in the murky depths of the cave?

Perhaps just long enough so that every single eye was riveted on that dark opening. And then, out of the deep, shadowy recesses within, there appeared a mummy-like figure "wrapped with strips of linen, and a cloth around his face" (11:44). Was there a collective gasp? Did some of the mourners swoon to the ground in a faint? Was everyone frozen into place, temporarily paralyzed by the shock of seeing something that *just couldn't be?* Dead men don't come back to life! But Lazarus did! At the command of the One Who is the Resurrection and the Life, he appeared at the entrance of the tomb![10]

After all the pain and suffering and anguish and doubt and resentment and misunderstanding and tears, God answered the sisters' unspoken prayer! Although Jesus had not come when they had thought He would, He had restored Lazarus to health. In His own time and in His own way, God answered abundantly beyond what they could have thought to ask for![11] Beyond their wildest dreams! Their brother was raised from the dead!

At long last, Martha understood! God's purpose was made clear! God's power and glory and *love* were revealed! And the grief-stricken plea wrenched from her broken heart was abundantly answered! Jesus was all she needed! Jesus was enough!

Praise God! Hallelujah! Give Him all the glory!

And if He can raise Lazarus from the dead after four days of being in the tomb, what do you think He cannot do for you or me?[12] What miracle do you think is beyond His power to accomplish?

One day that same Voice is going to thunder with a loud command, "and the dead in Christ will rise"![13] Regardless of whether our bodies have been buried for four days or a thousand years, regardless of whether they have been . . .

> burned at the stake,
> or eaten by wild animals,
> or frozen in an avalanche,
> or sunk in the ocean,
> or displayed in a velvet-lined casket,
> or entombed in a mausoleum,
> or sprinkled in the wind,

one day He will call us forth from the dead, and we will rise again! Praise God! Praise God! *Praise God!* All of our suffering will be over, and God Himself " 'will wipe every tear from their eyes. There will be no more death or mourning or crying or pain, for the old order of things has passed away.' He who was seated on the throne said, . . . 'Write this down, for these words are trustworthy and true.' "[14]

When you don't understand why, just trust Him!

Trust Him!
Trust Him!
Trust Him when you don't understand!
Trust His heart!
Trust His purpose!
Trust Him when your heart is broken!
Trust His goodness!
Trust Him beyond the grave!
Trust Him to know best!
Trust His plan to be bigger than yours!
Trust Him to keep His Word!
Trust Him to be on time!
Trust Him to be enough!
Trust Him to set you free!
Just trust God — and God alone!

When I don't understand why, I trust Him because . . .

God is *enough.*

Epilogue:
Why Won't God
Release Me
from the Pain?

Trusting God to Set Me Free

Now the Lord is the Spirit,
and where the Spirit of the Lord is,
there is freedom.

— 2 CORINTHIANS 3:17

Therefore,
there is now no condemnation
for those who are in Christ Jesus,
because through Christ Jesus
the law of the Spirit of life set me free
from the law of sin and death.

— ROMANS 8:1–2

Lazarus had been raised from the dead! But in the stunned silence, as he stood bound in the tomb's entrance with everyone staring at him in shocked consternation, it was obvious something was drastically, seriously wrong! He couldn't walk! And Martha couldn't enjoy having him back in her life!

Lazarus was bound tightly by the grave clothes — strips of linen that wound round and round him until he looked like a living mummy. The trappings of his death and Martha's grief surrounded him. Although he was alive, he could not walk in his new life. Lazarus needed to be set free . . . but he couldn't help or unwrap himself.

And so once again, Jesus could be heard giving Martha a clear, specific command:

"Take off the grave clothes and let him go" (11:44).

Has God worked a miracle in your marriage or your family or your health or your business? Has He finally answered your prayer after years and years of delay? But to your dismay, have you discovered that whatever or whomever you have prayed for is still bound and you are unable to enjoy the answer to prayer?

What grave clothes or bindings of death and grief surround your situation? Grave clothes can be . . .

memories of the past,
fear of the future,
uncertainty in the present . . .
lingering resentment,
an unforgiving spirit,
rooted bitterness . . .
an old relationship,
an old thought process,
a wrong attitude . . .
pride,
doubt,
selfishness.

Grave clothes will hinder your release from pain and grief. So let them go. *Let them go!* Deliberately, one by one, take them off.

If you are the one bound, it may mean you need someone to help unwrap you.

Someone who will pray specifically for you. Someone who will lead you into God's Word and teach you how to hear His voice speaking to you through it. Someone who can give you wise counsel. Someone who loves you enough . . . who cares enough . . . to honestly tell you what the grave clothes are that bind you. But you must let them go . . .

After years of marriage, a very precious friend recently discovered that while he had been patiently enduring his wife's criticism and lovingly trying to meet her demanding needs, she had had multiple affairs — some with his own "friends." His discovery of her infidelity came as she confessed it to him as part of her genuine repentance. In fact, for months he had noticed such a difference in her attitude and demeanor within the home that they had seemed to fall in love all over again. Their marriage at last seemed to be what he had so earnestly prayed for years that it would be. Their relationship had truly been "resurrected" into newness of life. But then she confessed what she had done! And the thrill of answered prayer and his joy in her were shattered! Although he could see she seemed to be truly transformed, the grave clothes of anger, bitterness, and unforgiveness were wound tightly around the marriage — and he refused to take them off and let them go. He clung to them, afraid that if he let them go, somehow she would get by with her sin. So he has filed for divorce.

And in the shadows, at the grave site of their marriage, with their relationship raised into newness of life and my friend refusing to unwrap it and let go of the . . .

resentment
and anger
and bitterness
and unforgiveness
and hurt
and pain,
I see tears on His face.

What wretched grave clothes are you clutching? Are they worth clinging to when they cause you to miss out on life? And love? And joy? And peace? And happiness? And freedom? *And total release from the pain?*

When God raised the Galatians from the dead, spiritually speaking, they clung to their old bindings of religiosity and legalism as they sought to live their new lives in Christ. They were limping and stumbling in their walk of faith while confused in their spirits with the attitude, *Why doesn't God release us?* So they were exhorted in words that you and I need to hear today: "It is for freedom that Christ has set us free. Stand firm, then, and do not let yourselves be burdened again by a yoke of slavery."[1]

The Galatians were exhorted to "not let yourselves be burdened." Freedom from the burden, release from the pain, was up to the Galatians! It was their choice!

Jesus Christ has set you and me free as surely as He raised Lazarus from the dead, but we have to take off the grave clothes *and let them go!*

How sad it would have been for Martha had she stopped short of going all the way in her obedience and refused to unwrap her brother. What a waste for Lazarus to be raised from the dead only to be unable to walk and enjoy his new life. How tragic if Lazarus had clutched the grave clothes to himself and refused to be unwrapped because they had become familiar and comfortable to him. How disastrous if Martha and Lazarus had both slipped into the habit of being accustomed to the bindings and settled for less than the life God intended for them to live!

The writer to the Hebrews exhorts us to throw off the grave clothes and "everything that hinders and the sin that so easily entangles, and let us run with perseverance the race marked out for us. Let us fix our eyes on Jesus."2 Jesus died on the Cross, but, praise God, He shed the grave clothes, and the Resurrection and the power and the glory followed!

Don't wallow in your "why's?"

Don't throw a pity party.

Don't remain in your misery.

Don't stop short of all God wants to do for you.

Understand that *you may not understand* this side of heaven.

Respect God's silences.

Claim through your own experience . . .
    the blessing that follows brokenness,
    the life that follows death,
and the glory that follows suffering!
Trust God to sort it all out in the end. He can break the bonds of your suffering — *now!* Trust Him! He will bring you through.

When I don't understand why, I trust Him because . . .

I want everything God has for me!

Notes

Why?
Trusting God When I Don't Understand

1. Jesus foretold the total destruction of Jerusalem when He revealed to His disciples that "not one stone here will be left on another; every one will be thrown down." (See Matthew 24:2. This prophecy was literally fulfilled in A.D. 70 when Rome destroyed Jerusalem and the temple within it.)

   In response to such an astounding revelation, the disciples blurted out a question: "When will this happen? . . . What will be the sign of . . . the end of the age?" (Matthew 24:3).

These are questions that believers throughout the ages have been grateful for because of the revelation His answer gives. In His response, Jesus described the last page of human history and listed characteristics that would be present in the generation that immediately precedes His second coming — characteristics that you and I are to watch for as signposts announcing His return.

The characteristics, or "signs of the times," as He had previously defined them, seem to fall into four categories: spiritual, national, personal, and environmental (see Matthew 16:3). While the "signs" in these categories have always been present in every generation, Jesus described them as birth pains — characteristics that will increase in frequency and intensity as the end of the world draws near (see Matthew 24:8). Just as birth pains seem to crescendo in an incredible climax of pain for the mother immediately prior to the actual delivery of the baby, so the signs of the times will climax in a time of intense human suffering that ushers in the "birth" of the kingdom of God on earth at the return of Jesus Christ.

Jesus painted a frightening picture of the days immediately preceding His return when He revealed that they would be a time of "great distress, unequaled from the beginning of the world until now — and never to be equaled again. If those days had not been cut short [by His return], no one would survive" (Matthew 24:21).

At times it seems the world is falling apart, but I know it's just falling into place as God arranges events in preparation for Jesus' return. If we are nearing the end of the age, you and I may be staring into a short-term future of intense, unprecedented, worldwide suffering.

2. See John 12:24.
3. See Romans 8:17.
4. See Jeremiah 18:1–6.
5. 2 Corinthians 4:7–10, 17.

Why Doesn't God Care?
Trusting God's Heart

1. See Genesis 3:15.

2. See 1 Peter 1:7.

Why Does God
Let Bad Things Happen?
Trusting God's Purpose

1. See Psalm 89:8.
2. See Romans 8:28.
3. See John 3:8.
4. See 1 Peter 1:6–9; 4:12–13, 19; Romans 8:28.

Why Me?
Trusting God When It's My Heart
That's Broken

1. See Luke 10:38; Matthew 21:17; and Mark 11:11–12. I have often wondered if Jesus feels as "at home" in my home as He did in theirs . . .
2. See Luke 10:41–42.
3. Ibid.
4. See John 12:1–11.
5. See Luke 18:18–23.
6. John 3:16.
7. Romans 5:8.

8. The four different rulers Daniel served under were: Nebuchadnezzar, emperor of Babylon (see Daniel 1:1–6); Belshazzar, emperor of Babylon (see Daniel 5); Darius, king of the Medes and Persians (see Daniel 5:30–31); and Cyrus, king of Persia (see Daniel 10:1).
9. See Daniel 6:25–27.

Why Is God Silent?
Trusting God's Goodness

1. Genesis 3:1.
2. Larry Crabb, *Finding God* (Grand Rapids, Mich.: Zondervan, 1993), 89.
3. Genesis 3:5.

Why Did God Let the Worst Happen?
Trusting God Beyond the Grave

1. When Jesus received the message, He was in the Transjordan, a day's journey from Bethany. So if the messenger took one day to get to Jesus, and Jesus delayed

for two days then took one more day to travel to Bethany, a total of four days had passed between the time the messenger left Bethany to inform Jesus and Jesus' actual arrival in Bethany. When He did arrive in Bethany, He was told that Lazarus had been dead four days (11:17). Apparently, Lazarus had died shortly after the messenger left Bethany to go to Jesus in the Transjordan.

Why Did God Do *That?*
Trusting God to Know Best

1. Habakkuk 1:2–3.
2. See Habakkuk 1:12–17.
3. See Joshua 5:13–6:20.
4. See Judges 6–7.
5. The disciples made another common mistake. They were basing their recommendation not to go to Jerusalem on the circumstances of Lazarus's health, not on the will of God. In other words, "Lord, if he sleeps, he will get better. Therefore, we don't need to go." The necessity of going to Jerusalem was not determined by Lazarus's condition but by God's will.
6. 1 John 4:7.

7. Matthew 7:1.
8. Romans 8:28.
9. Hebrews 6:14.

Why Doesn't God Protect Those He Loves?
Trusting God's Plan to Be Bigger Than Mine

1. Isaiah 63:9.
2. 2 Corinthians 12:8–10.
3. 1 Peter 1:6–7.
4. 1 Peter 1:8–9.
5. *Decision* magazine, September 2002, 8.

Why Hasn't God Answered My Prayer?
Trusting God to Keep His Word

1. Isaiah 43:1–4.
2. Daniel 3:17–18.
3. Daniel 3:24–25.
4. Psalm 23:4.
5. See Hebrews 11:6.
6. James 1:6–7.
7. See Matthew 17:20.

8. *Daily Light* is presently published by J Countryman, a division of Thomas Nelson, Nashville, Tennessee, 1998, under my name.

9. *Daily Light* combines portions of Scripture verses into morning and evening readings. The morning reading for March 6 is drawn from Proverbs 2:8; Psalm 37:23–24; Psalm 34:19; Psalm 1:6; Romans 8:28; 2 Chronicles 32:8; and Zephaniah 3:17 NKJV.

10. The cancer had not metastasized as feared and was successfully removed in surgery. Although Jonathan had a violent reaction to the follow-up radiation, he has passed his five-year benchmark for being cancer free with flying colors of good health, for which we continually praise God!

Why Didn't God Intervene?
Trusting God to Be on Time

1. Thomas Merton, *The Seven Storey Mountain* (New York: Harcourt, Brace & World, 1948), 75.

2. "A Final Goodbye," *People* magazine, 5 May 2003, 166.

Why Hasn't God Met My Needs?
Trusting God to Be Enough

1. See Romans 3:23.
2. See Romans 6:23.
3. See 2 Corinthians 5:8.
4. See 1 Corinthians 15:54–57.
5. See Revelation 2:11; 20:6, 14; and 21:8.
6. See Job 19:26; 1 Thessalonians 4:13–18.
7. See Psalm 56:8 KJV.
8. See Isaiah 63:9.
9. It has been suggested that one reason Jesus wept was that He knew the glory of where Lazarus was in comparison with where he would be when he returned to his earthly life. And although Jesus did raise Lazarus from the dead, Lazarus would die again.

Why Doesn't God Perform a Miracle?
Trusting God Alone

1. This and the previous quotes are from "The Message of Miracles," *Time*, 10 April 1995, 64–73.

2. This is a quote I pulled from the bulletin of Pawley's Island Baptist Church in Pawley's Island, South Carolina, a congregation pastored by Bob Barrows.
3. James 2:17.
4. It's important to understand the difference in *belief, faith,* and *trust.* "You believe that there is one God. Good! Even the demons believe that — and shudder" (James 2:19). James was pointing out that while the demons believed, they lacked faith — and certainly trust. Hebrews 11:6 says, "Without faith it is impossible to please God." And 1 John 5:4 assures us, "Everyone born of God overcomes the world. This is the victory that has overcome the world, even our faith." While faith pleases God and gives us victory that overcomes the world, heartfelt trust in Him brings us peace as all of our strivings cease and we simply rest in Him.
5. See John 9:1–7.
6. See John 5:1–9.
7. See Luke 6:6–10.
8. If Jesus wasn't embarrassed to pray in public and in front of hostile people, why are you and I embarrassed to pray

before a meal in our homes? Or at a restaurant table before we begin our meal? Or before presenting God's Word in Sunday school?

9. It has been said that Jesus called Lazarus by name because if He had simply said, "Come forth!" *all* the dead would have been raised!

10. Out of all the people buried in Judea, why did Jesus choose to raise Lazarus and not others? I've heard this story used to explain the Calvinistic doctrine that some people are predestined to be raised to eternal life while others are not. It may be that the doctrine can be argued from other passages of Scripture, but I reject that reasoning based on this story. It is very obvious from this passage that Lazarus was raised from the dead because his two sisters beseeched Jesus for help.

11. See Ephesians 3:20–21.

12. See Ephesians 1:18–21.

13. 1 Thessalonians 4:16.

14. Revelation 21:4–5.

Epilogue:
Why Won't God
Release Me from the Pain?
Trusting God to Set Me Free

1. Galatians 5:1.
2. Hebrews 12:1–2.